GOOD ENOUGH ISN'T

THE COLIN READ STORY

Good luck

Coli Read 3/19

Written by Paul Cheshire

ISBN: 978-1-5272-3073-6

Edited and designed by:
Book of My Life Ltd
20 Clyde Terrace
London
SE23 3BA
020 8133 6588
bookofmylife.co.uk

Additional editing by John Garley

Book OF MY Life

Philip, Jonathan, Colin & Norma

*This book is dedicated to my loving wife Norma and sons
Philip and Jonathan, who together made Podington Garden
Centre one of the best in the world*

Preface

Towards the end of a video released in 1996 to celebrate the Read family's successful garden centre business, Colin Read faces the camera and declares the centre "a plants person's paradise". He goes on to stress the key watchwords of "choice, service, quality and value", adding, "In fact, one of my mottoes is 'Good enough isn't.'"

Friends and family will be familiar with this phrase. They will also recognise that it encapsulates what Colin has been, and continues to be, all about, not least in his approach to work.

"The term itself did not become part of my vocabulary until several decades after I'd started work," he explains. "I'd always had the same feelings, I just hadn't expressed them in that particular way." Then, in the 1980s, he decided to enter a national business federation competition.

Colin takes up the story: "Hundreds of people eventually entered this competition, which required you to submit a phrase or saying that, more than any other single phrase, helped define your business. The prize for the winner was £20,000 to be spent on a marketing project.

"It didn't take long to come up with 'Good enough isn't'. For me, those people who say 'That's good enough' usually don't mean it. They're just admitting that they haven't achieved what they should or could have done. 'Good enough isn't' puts all I believe is important into a few simple words, into a term that's better than any other."

The phrase proved to be a winner. Podington Garden Centre was awarded the competition's first prize, which Colin decided to spend on a project called Gardening for Schools, promoting gardening to young people. This included giving tours, talks and organising 'garden in a seed tray' competitions, which proved highly popular with local schools.

Colin knew what the title of this book would be long before a word was written. As he says, it sums up his outlook on life. Far more than a promotional motto, the phrase has defined Colin's approach to his life as well as to his work. In the happy times and the sad, in sickness and in health, today, as always, for Colin Read it's still the case that 'Good enough isn't'.

Colin at 11 years old in the Cubs

Boyhood in Bletchley

Of course, in the late 1930s, and throughout the 1940s, the concept of 'Good enough isn't' was a long way in the future as these were the carefree days of Colin Read's childhood, a time for the most part coloured, though not clouded, by World War II.

Home was in Brooklands Road, Bletchley, a quiet road linking Bletchley Road (now Queensway) with Water Eaton Road. Generally the road contained houses, with log storage as well and a nursery growing tomatoes and other crops.

Born on 30 November 1935, Colin, with his mother Marion, father Walter and, later, younger sister Susan, lived at number 44, a three bedroom, red-brick terraced house also known as Glendene. Colin's father was born at 25 Brooklands Road. Colin's mum and dad had moved up the road to number 44 just before he was born.

"The only real difference between it then and now is that we didn't have an indoor bathroom. The toilet was outside and our bath was a tin one which we used in the kitchen right in front of the fire," recalls Colin.

Meanwhile, beyond the confines of 44 Brooklands Road, the little Buckinghamshire town of Bletchley was dominated by the railways, with the town's station just a few hundred yards from the Reads' home.

The railways loomed large in the life of the town and in the Read family—both Colin's dad, Walter, and Walter's father, Charlie, were train drivers. As Colin says, his father was "a very proud engine driver" who was at the throttle of trains running to and from Bletchley, a major rail junction on the West Coast line which carried people and freight between Scotland and London.

Working mostly local journeys, taking in other mainline railway towns such as Nuneaton and Crewe, Walter Read also ventured into London. Exempted from front-line service during the war, as train drivers provided a necessary and protected service, Colin's father frequently took trains to and from the capital during this period. Of course, as German aircraft regularly dropped bombs on London, this could be a risky business. On one occasion a bomb exploded close by as Walter steamed into Euston station.

Luckily the station wasn't hit. "Dad always used to say, 'Oh, I'll be all right, don't you worry about me,'" recalls Colin. "My mum must have been worried about what might happen to my dad though, but she kept her worries to herself."

One morning, the young lad joined his father and his fireman colleague on-board one of the steam engines—a rare treat. When Colin looked around the cabin he noticed a shovel. As he took a closer look, he saw the remnants of his dad and his mate's bacon-and-egg breakfast. They had cooked it on the shovel in the blazing heat of the engine's fire!

Some years later, Walter would witness the arrival of diesel locos, and while he made the switch to driving diesel trains, in his heart steam was still king.

"He accepted it, the conversion," says Colin, "but he preferred steam. He liked the feeling of the power he had over a steam train."

During Colin's boyhood, the presence and impact of trains and train-related business was obvious to anyone living or working in and around Bletchley. In complete contrast were the clandestine carryings-on which, at the end of the 1930s, had begun to unfold just a stone's throw from the station.

There had been a mansion at Bletchley Park for more than 200 years when, in 1938, a group of men calling themselves Captain Ridley's Shooting Party came to visit with a view to buying the country house and the attached 58 acres of land. At the head of this party was one Admiral Sir Hugh Sinclair, the head of the Secret Intelligence Service. He organised payment of the £6,000 asking price for the estate that would become a key, and highly hush-hush, hub of British code-breaking operations throughout the course of World War II.

While few of Bletchley's 5,000-plus residents had any inkling of what was going on at the place known in intelligence circles as Station X, locals in the wartime years did, of course, see the comings and goings of the men and women deployed to work there. In fact, many of them were billeted in nearby homes, including 44 Brooklands Road.

"When war was declared I was not yet four," Colin notes, "so I don't have many memories from the early days of World War II, but I do have a very clear memory of the ladies that were billeted with us."

With the family living in a compact house, taking in a lodger led to one big change in sleeping arrangements as, with no spare room, Colin and his little sister Susan were forced to share a bedroom. Having previously enjoyed the small luxury of his own room, Colin might have resented this change. Happily, he took the switch in his stride as "it seemed the right thing to do".

One of the first bed-and-breakfast lodgers was Miss Rubinstein, who Colin believes was related to the famous pianist, Arthur Rubinstein. An upper-class, well-spoken young lady, she appeared quite aloof to Colin.

"She'd have breakfast with us and not speak. Then she'd go to work in a big car which would come and fetch her," says Colin. "Later, she'd be brought back to our house, have a meal with us and then go to her room. Very quiet all the time, she kept herself to herself."

And even when these tenants did speak, they never talked about their work. "I did ask once," Colin admits, "but Dad told me to shut up and not question them about what they did. And being a polite and obedient boy, I did what I was told."

Not all encounters with the Bletchley Park 'gals' were so frosty, though, especially where one friendly lady was concerned.

"Pat Bratt was very memorable," Colin recalls. "Another well-spoken woman, she came to stay with us, together with her red setter and a horse, which she stabled at a nearby garage." Colin has fond memories of this lodger, recounting how she'd happily spend time talking with him "not about her life but about me, really".

One day Pat was due to head off to work. Before departing, she said to Colin's mother, "I'm going to have to leave the dog with you today, Mrs Read."

Young Colin was at home that day. "Her red setter was the best-disciplined dog I've ever seen," he says. "Before Pat went to work that day, she turned to her pet and said, 'Dog, take your orders from this lady here!'. The lady she was referring to was my mum, and somehow the dog understood that order and so, throughout the morning, it did exactly what my mother told it to do!"

After a few hours, Colin said to his mother, "Can I take the dog to the shop, Mum? I've got some money on my coupon, so I can buy some sweets." His mother agreed. The shop, run by a man the children used to call Mr Bonbon, was just around the corner.

As Colin left, his mum said to the dog, "Go with Colin!" and it dutifully followed him to the shop. Once inside, young Colin did what most children love to do: he picked out the sweets he wanted to buy. What happened next is as clear to Colin today as the day it occurred.

"Mr Bonbon took the jelly beans, or whatever I'd chosen, and filled a paper bag with the sweets he got from a glass jar behind the counter. Giving him a coupon, I then left the shop and walked back home. Back at the house, my mother said, 'You've got your sweets then, Colin, but where's the dog?'"

"Oh, I told her to sit down outside the shop!" Colin replied. In a panic, he raced back. Happily, he found the dog still patiently sitting there—just as she'd been told to.

During Pat Bratt's stay, the red setter gave birth to a litter of puppies in the shed in the Reads' back garden. This shed was not the only outhouse of course. The garden was also home to the family's air-raid shelter, a makeshift Anderson unit—a tiny, cramped, damp-smelling affair dug into a large hole with a corrugated iron blast-wall and a rockery arranged on the roof.

"We were frightened when the German planes were about and dived into the air-raid shelter," Colin recalls.

On these occasions, the family would huddle together there until the siren sounded the all clear. The discomfort, however, was a small price to pay for their safety. Happily, the danger in Bletchley was not too great. German bombers did drop their bombs locally, but mostly they flew past carrying their deadly payloads to unleash on other towns, the Luftwaffe utterly ignorant of the enormous importance of the work taking place in this quiet, unassuming corner of England.

In addition to the overhead activity, down on terra firma nearby land was requisitioned, as Colin explains: "Opposite our home, which was a very modern house, were these terraced houses, and surrounding those was the place we used to call 'the logs'. It was a place where, during the war years, German POWs used to work amongst the willow trees and the lakes."

He continued, "We used to do a lot of playing around there and, surprisingly perhaps, we didn't see these prisoners as bad people because they befriended a lot of us. I got the impression that they were pleased to be there because they got better treatment as prisoners than they would've done fighting at the front."

This development of 'the logs' provided an exciting and exotic interest in Colin's young life, as he explains: "The men they brought to work prepared timber there, moving logs and cutting them up to provide wood for construction work. It was a busy site with what must have been about 50 or 60 POWs working there."

Although Colin and his friends didn't get to know any of the Germans by name, they did talk regularly with them. Friendly and "very nice", the men also made toys and other knick-knacks—fashioned from bits of wood and scraps of material—which they'd give to the local boys and girls.

Colin no longer has any of these toys but remembers some of them well. "One of these was made with a bit of string that hung down from a piece of wood, a bit like a table-tennis bat. You wound up the string and it spun around, round and round. They also gave us whistles and wooden flutes."

For all the wartime excitement and tensions, one of Colin's earliest memories is not of railways, lady lodgers or POWs, but of something much closer to home and a child's heart—Christmas.

"One of the first things I remember is my dad carrying a pillowcase up the staircase having just got back from the pub one Christmas Eve." Colin was four or five years old.

The little boy knew from previous Christmases that the pillowcase was likely to contain little treats like an apple or a pear and a cap gun.

"I remember waking up and seeing my father standing there. I still laugh at this now, seeing him in the small bedroom and him then saying 'Oh, blast it!'

"My mother said to him, 'Shh! You'll wake him up.'

"He said, 'It's okay, he was asleep.' But, of course, I wasn't asleep."

Father Walter (1906–1992)

A Bletchley boy, Walter, who was one of six children, the others being brothers Charles and Edward (known as Ted) plus sisters Maud, Minny and Nan, grew up in a house a stone's throw from the one Walter and his wife would eventually buy in Brooklands Road.

Colin remembers his grandmother, Walter's mum, as "a well-informed, nicely spoken, very helpful person", while Walter's dad, Charlie, born in 1888, was commonly referred to locally as a 'midwife good and true'.

This unusual title was bestowed upon him because, in 1921, he was one of those responsible for 'bringing into the world' Bletchley's new Working-men's Social Club and Institute Union.

The younger Charlie, like brother Walter, was yet another railwayman, who, during Colin's childhood years, lived in Lennox Road, Bletchley, with a garden Colin remembers as being "lovely". As for Colin's Uncle Ted, he was a prize-winning fisherman. For example, in July 1936

Ted was one of 102 competitors who entered his club's Individual Angling Championship, which was held in Newport Pagnell. Coming first, Ted's catch that summer's day weighed in at 3lbs 14oz and 12 drams—which was a full half-pound heavier than the weightiest fish hooked by his nearest rival.

A few weeks later, Ted Read scooped first prize for the second year in a row at Leighton Buzzard Athletic Club's annual championship, while in November that year he won that club's James Dance Cup for the third successive year.

As for Walter Read, he was a family man who made sure that good food was never in short supply, even during the years of rationing. There was always a ready supply of fresh home-grown produce—onions, spring onions, carrots, potatoes, beetroot and other vegetables—thanks to Walter.

"He used to clamp the root vegetables, either potatoes or carrots," Colin recalls, "put them in clamps and straw, and then, when they were fully grown, he'd take them out of the clamps and string up the onions so we had them available throughout the year.

"The onions were hung up in the larder. The larder wasn't that cold but, of course, we didn't have a refrigerator in those days." These vegetables would then be used as ingredients when Marian Read cooked family dinners.

Another by-product of Walter Read's passion for gardening was the interest it sparked in his son.

"My dad would spend hours in the garden and I used to join him, and before long I got to know how to grow things. I really enjoyed gardening, although I didn't realise, of course, that years later I'd be doing it for a living."

Away from his garden, Walter's great passion was football. He captained the local railway team, Bletchley LMS, which was then one of the best teams in the area, and as a young lad he'd been good enough to have trials with Chelsea and Arsenal.

Establishing himself as a fixture in the LMS side (for many seasons he was the team's centre half), Walter was a tough yet fair player, who never reacted whatever the provocation of opposing forwards. Not everyone was impressed, though, as one young Bletchley lad was only too happy to point out to Walter's son.

"Sometimes I'd go to see a film on Saturday mornings," recalls Colin. "One day, when I was at the cinema, a boy about my age came up to me and said, 'Hey, you! Your dad's Walter Read, isn't he?'

"I said, 'Yes, why?'

"'He keeps stopping my dad from scoring goals,' said the lad, adding some rather colourful language to the conversation.

"I said, rather proudly, 'Well in that case he's doing his job as a centre half isn't he?'".

After a long amateur football career—he was still playing until he was 40—Walter quit the game, turning his sporting talents to boxing, becoming the trainer at a local boxing club. This hobby carried on for a few years and, forever a sportsman, he took up snooker to pass his retirement days.

Walter passed away in 1992, but he left a lasting legacy with his son Colin.

Colin's mother & father at home in Bletchley

Mother Marian née Green (1908–1985)

Unlike Walter, Colin's mother Marian grew up not in Bletchley but ten or so miles from there in Cheddington, the Buckinghamshire village where, for many years, her parents ran the Swan pub, a traditional English inn complete with thatched roof. Both his mother's parents were still alive and kicking when Colin was a lad, and he has fond memories of visiting them back then,

"At that time they lived in a big place, a lovely detached house in Pitstone. Just by the railway line it was, and we'd walk the two-and-a-half to three miles there from Cheddington station.

"My grandmother was a very gentle lady and also a good cook. We had some fine times there and used to walk across the road from the house and go through the fields to the canal to swim in it or try to catch fish there."

In Colin's youth, his mother would make the journey from Bletchley to Cheddington and back once or twice a month—the same journey that, some years earlier, young Walter Read had made.

Heading off on his bike one evening, Walter had followed a similar route, cycling from his home in Bletchley to a dance in the village at which, that evening, he would meet his Maid Marian, the girl who would later become his wife.

Once married, Marian was happy to be a stay-at-home mother, looking after son Colin and, from 1938, Colin's sister Susan. Described by Colin as "a very proper, well-spoken and nice lady", Marian was never heard to swear and didn't take kindly to those who did.

After Susan arrived, it soon became apparent that the siblings were chalk and cheese. While the elder brother was, as Colin puts it, "a quiet, shy boy", Susan was "a jumping-about, noisy, showoff girl". Colin proudly admits that his sister had a real talent for getting on with other people though.

A close knit family, the Reads would enjoy country walks and ride bikes together. Their annual holidays too provided many happy moments. Taking full advantage of the free rail travel that came as a perk of Walter Read's job, each summer the parents and children would board a train and head for the seaside. "We'd spend one or two weeks somewhere at places like Rhyl and Llandudno," Colin recalls, "but my favourite holiday, the most memorable one, was spent in Blackpool. That was a special holiday what with the lights along the front, the famous ballroom, not to mention the beach, sea and all the other seaside fun and entertainment my sister and I were excited by and enjoyed."

Despite the free travel, like many working class families, the Reads didn't stay in hotels when they reached their holiday destination, instead preferring cheaper, more homely guest houses. Stories abound of such guest houses of the period being unwelcoming places run by forbidding landladies, but Colin's memories are of generous hostesses providing "big breakfasts and very, very good food".

The Cedars School, Leighton Buzzard, May 1952.
Colin top row third from the left

Colin Read's School Days

Still in existence today, Bletchley Road infants' school building was barely five years old when young Master Read first set eyes on it. At that time, the school grounds were surrounded by iron railings. However, soon after Britain had declared war on Germany, the railings were cut down as the country rounded up every scrap of metal to plough into the war effort.

Inside the school walls, the children's education was overseen by the headmistress, Mrs Wodhams. Born Isabella Noble Walker, she had eventually married a local coal-merchant, Charles Wodhams, the couple making their home in Church Street, close to the canal on the eastern edge of Bletchley. A woman of medium height, who died in 1945 aged 81, Mrs Wodhams was, therefore, already well into her seventies when Colin Read was a pupil at Bletchley Road infants' school. He recollects that Mrs Wodhams had a stern voice and was "a bit of a stickler for discipline". This authoritarian rule was put to the test on one particular occasion by young Colin.

"She used to have all the children line up each day in the hall for assembly, and on this day during assembly I put my hand up and asked if I could go to the toilet. Well, Mrs Wodhams didn't believe that I was a boy that needed to go to the toilet. She thought I was just one of those children looking to skive off. It took me some time to actually persuade her that I did need to go to the toilet and, eventually, she begrudgingly allowed me to go."

One other clear memory Colin still has of these early school days is of wartime ration books, in particular the family's clothing book, which contained additional coupons to be put towards extra-large shoes for the young boy of the household, shoes to fit feet which were bigger than those of any of his classmates!

Away from school, and despite the wartime restrictions, Colin and his playmates made merry and enjoyed themselves like children anywhere and whatever the circumstances. And on one particular occasion, a story his father had told him got young Colin into a spot of bother.

"My dad used to recall how he used to enjoy himself when he was a young boy and he let drop about pranks he used to play. One of these involved tying two door knockers together on next-door properties and then knocking on one and running off. You knocked on the door with the string tied to it, you see, so try as they might the door wouldn't open!" Colin notes, smiling at the memory of this mischievous mayhem.

"The fascination was that you would set this train of events in motion, a train going on and on. Anyway, one evening after we'd been tying knockers together, I was standing there in an alleyway nearby with my friend, Colin Tooth, when one of the homeowners who we'd played the prank on found us.

"She got really cross. We ran off but later that evening, when I was tucked up in bed, the doorbell rang. When my father opened the door, there was the lady from the alley, the one whose door knocker we'd tied string to. Straightaway she told Dad what we'd done, and how our prank had damaged the knocker. Well, my dad listened to what this angry woman had to say and then, calm as you

like, said, 'It can't have been him, he was in bed fast asleep.'"
If Colin thought that was the end of the matter, he was very much mistaken.

"He gave me a real telling off after that, and I said to him, 'Dad, you told me what to do.'

"He said, 'Yes, I did, but I didn't tell you to go and do it!'"

Such dressing-downs did little to dampen the boyish sense of adventure and fun that Colin still retains, and there's a glint in his eye when he tells his tale of apple scrumping.

"Down the road from where we lived there was a nursery, an old-fashioned fruit nursery, and the nurseryman's house was there as well, and, as you can imagine, the nursery orchard had lots of apple trees in it. And back then, during the war, apples were scarce. Well, my friends and I used to play cricket against the nursery's fence, and sometimes our ball would go over the fence. So then we'd knock on the nurseryman's door and say, 'Can we get our ball back, please, mister?'"

The nurseryman, being a kindly character, would let the boys in to find and fetch their ball, which they'd then take back outside along with their crop of secretly stashed apples.

War Ends, Secondary Education Begins

On 8 May 1945 the end of the war in Europe was celebrated throughout the British Isles. In London huge crowds, joyful and relieved, gathered in Trafalgar Square and outside Buckingham Palace, while elsewhere VE Day street parties were enjoyed as people of all ages, young and old, let their hair down. In Bletchley, nine-year-old Colin was at school when the end of World War II was announced.

"We were told that the war was over, and then we all rushed home and the street was closed off to traffic. There were tables out and we had a great party in our street. The kids wore paper hats and, even though there was rationing, we still had lots to eat and drink, and everyone was really happy."

One year later, in September 1946, Colin moved up to secondary school. In the 1940s, most boys and girls who attended Bletchley Road junior and infants school went on to the neighbouring senior school. Colin's sister Susan would later follow this route. Her brother, though, was awarded a scholarship to grammar school.

The circumstances surrounding this award are now lost in the mists of time. All Colin knows for certain is that he sat and passed an 11-plus exam to qualify for the scholarship he was awarded, although he doesn't remember doing so.

However hazy the path to that grammar school in Leighton Buzzard, Colin's time there is still clearly recalled. Fronting Church Square at one end of the High Street, the school's main building had previously been the Georgian home of Mary Norton, the children's author of *The Borrowers* books and *Bonfires and Broomsticks*, which was the basis for the 1960s film *Bedknobs and Broomsticks*. The young Kathleen Pearson (as she was then known) lived at The Cedars until 1921, the year Bedfordshire County Council bought the property for about £4,000 and created Cedars School.

Just over a quarter of a century later, Colin, together with best friend Colin Tooth, became one of the first pupils of the newly named Cedars Grammar School, this son of a train driver making the short journey to and from school by rail.

Just like his primary school, Cedars was attended by boys and girls. However, at the new school the sexes were kept strictly separate, on the same site but schooled in different buildings.

This was just one of the major changes Colin had to adapt to. "It was different to what I was used to. More strict, and with a headmaster, Mr Broad, who wouldn't think twice about taking his cane to your backside!"

Though quickly adjusting to secondary school rules and regulations, surprisingly perhaps given his scholarship background young Master Read did not turn out to be an all-round scholar. He was excellent at mathematics and woodwork, but the other subjects did not really interest him.

This proved a source of frustration for at least one teacher. "The lady who taught Latin, who stood there in front of the class with her hair tied in a bun," Colin explains, "just couldn't for the life of her understand why someone like me, who was really good at maths, arithmetic and algebra, wasn't good at Latin because, in her mind, she thought the brain of a mathematician was perfectly configured to excel at Latin."

Other teachers were more understanding. "The maths master and the science master were very strict, but because I was good I got on quite well with them."

Generally then, young Colin kept out of trouble, although there was one occasion when he ended up being caned. He doesn't remember the incident that led to this painful punishment, just that it was brought about by "somebody else's mistake".

Another unpleasant recollection of those grammar school days concerned a visit to the school dentist.

"I'm reminded of that every day because there's a gap between my back teeth where he pulled about three or four teeth out. To this day I can still picture that dentist. He was a nice enough guy but, *yank, yank!* Just pulled the teeth out!"

Colin can't recall the name of this particular exponent of the dentist's art, but he does remember the family's own dentist, a Mr Marshall, who was none too impressed by his fellow practitioner's handiwork. As another dentist later confirmed, the school dentist should have done something else, something less drastic and less long lasting.

Tales of a severe Latin mistress, caning and tooth extractions should not give the impression, though, that Master Read's lot at Cedars was a grim one. Far from it, especially away from the classrooms (and the dentist's chair). The woodwork room was a favourite haunt.

Wood was still scarce in the immediate post-war years, but that didn't stop Colin, who'd beg or borrow bits of timber, which he'd saw, plane and piece together to make various items. One of his largest, most ambitious projects was taken on when he was 15 years old.

"I think at the time my mum was quite frustrated that she hadn't got enough cupboard space. It was a small kitchen," he adds. "So I told her I'd make some new furniture.

At school I'd made all sorts of bits and pieces, knew about making things, and so for our kitchen I made everything. I put together doors using two-by-one frameworks on which I affixed hardboard sheets using little tacks and glue. I made the worktop, too, which I laminated with Formica."

At a time when most British homes still had traditional free-standing units, Colin reckons the finished fit-out, which also included a Belfast sink with teak surround, was "the talk of the town".

Along with woodwork, sport was a prime passion. No surprise this given Colin's father's love of football and boxing. As things turned out, though, the son's sporting interests were very different. As with many grammar schools, the main winter game was rugby union, but one terrible and sad incident confirmed to Colin that this was not the sport for him.

Standing on the touchline one afternoon, he was watching older boys playing rugby when, all of a sudden, a run-of-the-mill game took a tragic turn. Tackled by an opponent, one player—the school's head boy—suffered a broken neck. He died from his injury.

"I said to myself, I'm not going to play that game. I didn't want to before I saw this boy killed. Afterwards, I was determined I wouldn't play rugby ever again."

Instead, he turned his attention to two non-contact sports: swimming and running. His love of swimming took hold despite the somewhat basic facilities of the local outdoor pool. The water was cold and the changing area was just as unwelcoming. On one particular cold and windy morning, Colin decided he wasn't going to swim that day.

"We were almost at the poolside when I just said to myself, it's too cold to swim. I told the teacher, 'I'm not going in that pool, sir, I am not going in!'

"He said, 'You get in there, Read' but I refused and then just took off, running round the school grounds. Well, the teacher then got the rest of the class to chase me. But they couldn't catch me."

A good swimmer, who "won all the swimming prizes", Colin was also a fast runner. Later, as he became more interested in running, he joined Bletchley Athletic Club, whose home was in Denbigh Road, near what is today the home ground of Milton Keynes Dons FC.

Specialising in cross-country, Colin raced and won at various local meets. One of these was in the small Bedfordshire town of Stotfold.

The race there proved to be 16-year-old Colin's finest hour 'in the country' as he led the six-mile event from the front to win comfortably. He'd hit upon the idea for this front-running tactic after seeing that the 200 or so runners were expected to pass through a small gate at the far end of a farmer's field.

"I thought that if I got stuck by that gate with all the other runners, I'd never win," Colin recalls. "So when the starting gun went, I shot off and went through the gate about ten yards ahead of everybody else.

"Good job I did too because they all got held up there. Jammed up it was. I'd been sure before the race started that I'd do all right, but once I'd reached that gate in the lead I was pretty sure then that I'd win. I've still got the medal I was given that day!"

Another triumphant race day followed a short time later when Colin took part in his final school sports day. "It was the last time I really ran seriously," Colin says. "And I finished in style, winning the 220 and 440-yard races, as well as the mile race—and all on the same day."

Away from the cross-country courses and athletics tracks, Colin was a member of the school's Army Training Corps, in addition to belonging to a local scout troop, and he well remembers the many ATC parades he took part in. As a scout, he ended up becoming a troop leader and was awarded a distinctive scouting badge.

"It was a big wide badge with a red cross on it, and if you were given one of those badges it meant that you were experienced in first aid."

Being a scout also gave boys the opportunity to enjoy camping trips, sleeping under canvas in faraway outposts like Windermere in the Lake District.

Meanwhile, back home in Bletchley there were birds—tall, slim Yorkshire canaries—to be looked after, as Colin explains: "I used to like keeping caged birds, which I got locally from a man called Mr Wait, who was the champion canary producer in the area. I'd got talking to him one day and he ended up selling me some. I set up a little breeding colony—just four pairs—and kept them in the back garden in my dad's shed, the same shed Pat Bratt's dog had had her puppies in during the war."

A Fateful Meeting

His teenage years also saw Colin take on a paper round, a first small step into the world of work and a paid job that was to have lifelong consequences. "I took on a Sunday paper round because the weekday train journeys to and from school didn't leave me enough time for a morning round. The round I did get took four hours to complete because I not only had to deliver papers but also collect customers' payments. Taking so long upset the people at the end of the round, though, because they used to get their papers so late in the day."

There were other customers, however, who were pleased to see Colin and vice versa, with one in particular really catching his eye. Colin explains: "There was one house I had to call on in North Crescent, Bletchley, near to the Oxford to Cambridge railway line, and before long I happened to notice an attractive girl who lived in one of the houses there. She'd take the papers from me at the door. Of course, I had no idea then what was going to happen in the future."

This customer was Norma Lewtas, the girl who, years later, Colin would marry, and the couple would go on to enjoy a lifetime together as Mr and Mrs Read.

Away from the world of work, there was plenty of socialising to be enjoyed with an early venue being the local young person's dance club.

"My friend Colin Tooth and I would go there," the other Colin states, "and we mostly just sat there. In fact, we didn't really like the place, so when one of us said 'Let's go along to one of the Labour League of Youth meetings' that was it; we starting going to those instead."

Soon Colin came across a familiar face at meetings above the Co-op shop in Albert Street, Bletchley, and Colin's life would never be the same.

"I was there with my mates when this young lady walked by. (I later learned that she had started the Labour League of Youth in Bletchley.) I took one look and realised that this was Norma, the pretty girl I used to see on my paper round, so I said hello—and the rest is history."

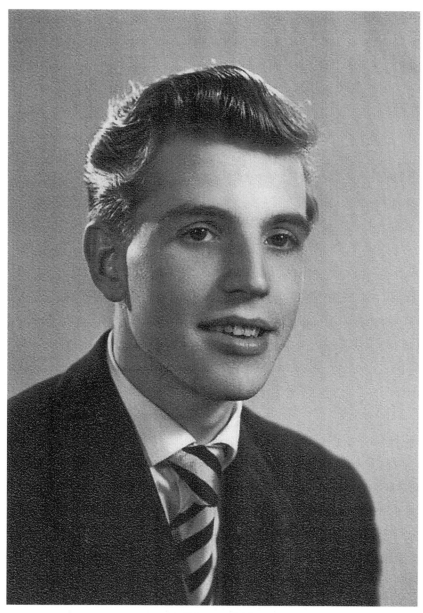

Colin aged 19

In & Out of Work

A short time later, Colin's school days came to an end. Leaving Cedars aged 16, he quit the world of education to take up his first full-time job.

"I wanted to be an architect," Colin states. "I liked design and still do." But at 17 and with just two O levels to his name—predictably one in maths, the other in woodwork—ambitions to follow in the footsteps of Le Corbusier and the other architectural masters he admired had to be shelved. So it was that, with national service on the not-too-distant horizon, Colin started looking for work. Applying for jobs, one organisation that really appealed as a potential employer was the Ordnance Survey. But turned down by OS, Colin joined his father as a fellow employee of the by then nationalised London Midland Region railway company, starting work there as a land surveyor.

"I liked the idea of surveying in foreign countries, in Africa and other exotic locations, but the railways here in England also offered plenty of scope for travelling."

Finding his talents well matched to the assignments he was given, Colin took to his new job straightaway.

"I shone there, even though all the drawings and all the measurements in those days were still made using old-fashioned methods," Colin reveals.

Within a few months, Colin was being sent out on his own "very important jobs".

Unfortunately, it wasn't long before he was called up for national service, which, in the immediate post-war years, every able-bodied British male who was between the ages of 17 and 21 and not a registered conscientious objector had to go through. Then aged 18, Colin was duly conscripted and headed to nearby Cardington to enrol.

A Brief Encounter with National Service

Colin was billeted at Cardington airfield for an introductory week, or as he puts it, "I was given a haircut and told to say 'Yes, corporal'." From the first he disliked the regimented aspects of military life, although he had been fortunate to be granted his first choice of serving with the RAF, the vast majority of other national-service conscripts finding themselves assigned to two-year stays in the army.

The induction period concluded, it was off for training to West Kirby, a pretty little seaside village on the Wirral peninsula at the mouth of the River Dee. Colin had little chance to explore the town or its beach as, like the many other thousands of new recruits to pass through the RAF training camp at nearby Larton, he soon embarked on an intensive time of square-bashing, marching, daily PE, kit preparation and polishing, all under the watchful eye of demanding non-commissioned officers (better known as NCOs).

Colin had set his heart on becoming a pilot. However, not long after entering the camp via its gates on Saughall Massie Road, he'd changed tack, opting to qualify as a navigation officer.

"I did want to be a pilot, but they wouldn't let me train to be one unless I committed myself to more than three years' training. Instead, I decided I'd be a navigator as the qualifications and the skills I had at that time seemed well suited to the role. The RAF agreed, and I was taken on as a potential navigation officer."

Taking this route also meant that he'd only have to serve the minimum two years' national service. Barely had his time at West Kirby begun, though, when Colin was learning just how tough or otherwise life in an RAF training camp could be. Still a young man, Colin, quickly learned how to survive—and thrive—in his new surroundings.

"I wasn't manipulative, but I tried to keep to the middle of the road when things did happen. I was also aware of the games the NCOs would play on the more naïve recruits," he says. "For example, a lad went up to an officer one time and asked 'What do I do with this rubbish, sir?' and was told to put it in a bin outside.

"So he did this, only for two other officers to come along and ask, 'Who put this rubbish in this bin?' Well, when the boy owned up, they shouted at him to take the rubbish out of the bin and paint it all white. And they pulled that stunt three times in one day!"

Of course, there was no escaping some of the more onerous chores, such as shovelling coal for hours on end into tanks, but there were far less arduous jobs too as Colin was lucky enough to find out early on in his time at West Kirby.

"I was sent to work in the stores, so off I trotted not knowing what to expect. When I got there, I knocked on the door of the squadron leader who was running the stores.

"Come in!" a voice on the other side says. So in I went, and as soon as I entered the squadron leader barks out, 'Take your hat off!'

"'Yes, sir,' I replied and sat down, and he told me what he expected of me.

"'I want a cup of tea at ten o'clock, a cup of tea at two o'clock and you go at four!'

"'Oh, right,' I mumbled, and that's exactly what I did, and every day I'd come back to the barracks all bright and breezy while the others would be absolutely worn out! You see, nobody had an easier job than I did."

However, this phase of camp life didn't last long as Colin soon fell ill, just a month into training. Initially it seemed as though he'd picked up a heavy cold. This was not the case.

"In fact, I was actually going down with pneumonia. One minute I was parading with the others but then, when the corporal commanded us to stand to attention, I collapsed in a heap on the floor."

The irony of the situation was, therefore, that instead of a life spent training to be a navigator and sharing mess life with 20 or so other men in their primitive wooden barracks, Colin was confined to bed in the camp sickbay. For some young men this would have been a depressing, even worrying, experience, but this is not how Colin remembers it.

"Other people in that platoon probably saw me as someone who was suffering because of my illness. But it didn't work out like that for me. Not at all. In fact, I had a fantastic time in the sickbay!"

A rich cast of patients played a significant part in making Colin's convalescence so pleasant, as did the presence of the female nursing staff. Fun and laughter were never far from the surface, some of it enjoyed at the expense of the nurses.

"The matron and the nurses would make their rounds every day, handing out medicines, changing bedlinen etc in a ward full of young male patients. Well, the bloke next to me, he was such a character. The nurses would be moving around, bending over and generally going about their business while behind their backs my mate and the other blokes would be making remarks and gestures, leering and pulling faces, joking and laughing and so on," Colin remembers with a smile.

Of course, matron and the nurses knew exactly what was going on and would take the 'banter' in their stride. As Colin says, "They'd try to keep a straight face among all these blokes who were making fun of them, and say things to the men like 'What are you laughing at?'"

The fellow in the next bed to Colin not only made him laugh, he also cut him in on an enjoyable extra-curricular activity. "This guy seemed to know everything that was going on, and he introduced me to the bookmaker who used to come round the ward."

Basic national service wages were meagre—28 shillings (£1.40) a week compared to an average weekly wage at that time of more than £8, so for many conscripts the opportunity to boost income by having a flutter was too good to turn down. Colin can't be sure but reckons the commanding officers at the West Kirby training camp must have turned a blind eye to the bookie's on-site presence.

"I think he must have been allowed to visit the ward because he did it openly. I never took it seriously, the gambling, but I'd put a few bob on the horses each week."

Of course, the good times in the camp sickbay did not last. Colin recovered quickly from his bout of pneumonia—helped by a daily issue of a bottle of Guinness—and was discharged after a stay of three to four weeks. There was to be no immediate return to life in the barracks, though, as he was promptly sent home on a month's leave as part of the recuperation process.

Then, shortly after his return to West Kirby, the would-be navigator found himself up in front of a three-man panel, with the state of his health having put his national service future in the balance.

"They said I had a 'weak stomach', and that meant I couldn't be allowed to fly. I needed to be healthier than I was otherwise they couldn't rely on me. So there I was on my own before these three officers sitting on a bench in front of me," Colin remembers.

"Three officers, two options: pay corps or out!"

With the stark choice of processing wages and completing staff payslips or leaving the RAF, the exchange that followed was brief.

"Do you want to go away and think about it?" one officer asked.

"No, I'll take the option to leave," Colin replied.

Hurrying back to Bletchley, Colin could not contain his delight when his parents opened the front door to find their son before them.

"I'm out! I'm out!"

Working for the Railways, Part Two

Back in Bletchley after his short but eventful time undertaking national service, Colin wasted no time in securing paid employment again, soon re-joining the London Midland Region company but in a different role second time around.

"When I went back to work for LMR I had a meeting with Mr Denute, the head of the land surveying department. Well, there must have been something clever about me then because I was thinking ahead. Anyway, I told Mr Denute that I really wanted to get qualified as a chartered surveyor. He had no problem with this but told me the only way I could do that was to change departments."

Happy to do so, Colin joined the railway company's land surveying team in London, working in the same office block, right by Euston station, in which he'd worked during his previous stint with LMR. He'd enjoyed his earlier time in the capital, frequently walking the streets of London during his lunch hours and other free time, doing what he calls his "visual surveys" of the city's great buildings in Kensington and beyond. Of course, as a surveyor his job regularly took him away from London, the memories of two particular field trips staying with him down the decades. One of these saw him take the train to North Wales, the other a train to Liverpool.

"I was sent on jobs to survey scenes, producing drawings of the area for whatever reason. Building a new station, track re-laying or whatever. I used to do the survey. And for one particular project I was sent to Blaenau Ffestiniog.

"I'd never heard of the place and didn't know where it was, but I got off the train at Llandudno and got on a second one to Blaenau Ffestiniog, the tracks going up and up for quite a long way and the train slowly ascending... *chug, chug, chug*. And I was on the train on my own and I'd never seen such a beautiful landscape in my life before. I have since, in Norway, but that February day in Wales the snow was covering all the land and I was awestruck.

"It was an undulating, heavily mountainous area and there were all these snowed-over slag heaps. Even they looked beautiful to me that day. I just couldn't believe how attractive it all was."

While the journey through this part of Snowdonia, with its slate mines and mountains, was memorable, the job Colin was due to work on out in that superbly scenic location ended up being postponed.

"I was met at the station by two 'chain men', as they were called, a couple of old boys who'd been told to help me measure stuff and so on. But the top and bottom of it was that the work didn't take place as I got a call from head office telling me to come home due to the wintry weather.

"So I slept in the station hotel overnight and then came back south the next day. No work but a very interesting trip. What I'd seen was totally different to anything I'd seen and I was so impressed by the landscapes I'd viewed."

Colin's working trip to Liverpool around this same time was also memorable, but for very different reasons.

"I needed to go and survey some sidings in Liverpool, but the sidings were so congested with engines constantly on the move—in and out—that I decided, in my wisdom, to go outside on to the nearby street to do some of the measuring from there. I would then measure off that into the work so it was more accurate.

"I had one or two old boys, plate layers they were, to help me. Plate layers were the people that used to inspect and maintain the railway tracks, but these men, I got them to carry the kitbag containing the string, rope, the measuring tapes and everything else such as chains. So there we were, banging a nail in the pavement on some street or other, and then we'd set off to the next point and then the next. We'd triangulate and then carry out the next measurements."

Colin doesn't recollect why the three of them were surveying this area in and around these Liverpudlian sidings, but he remembers very clearly what occurred while they were doing this work.

"We were establishing a base line and taking measurements off it out on the street with our 100-foot tape, and at one point we were working not far from a bus stop."

Happening to look over at a bus that was stationary at this end-of-the-line stop, Colin was mortified to see a man step off this bus and grab the work bag that had been left at the roadside while the measuring work took place nearby. The opportunist thief then jumped back on to the bus, which immediately began to move off, swiftly pursued by Colin, the former schoolboy running ace.

"Luckily, it was a busy Liverpool street, so busy that the bus couldn't get up any speed because of all the other vehicles. Nevertheless, I still had to weave in and out of the moving traffic to reach the bus. Then, when I caught up with it, I jumped on board and found the bloke who'd stolen my bag, shouted 'You rotten thief!' and, with all the passengers on the bus cheering and clapping, I snatched my bag back!"

A good tale with a happy ending and, as Colin stresses with a smile on his face, "It's a true story."

Back in London the LMR offices close to Euston station housed a 20-strong workforce. In the mid-1950s there were no computers, photocopiers, printers or even calculators. The surveyor's lot was a labour-intensive one, requiring the drawing up of numerous plans and surveys which featured imperial measurements—yards, feet and inches—and costings in pounds, shillings and pence.

Much of the basic preparation of these bills of quantities was delegated to Colin, the office junior, with various calculations and copying to be carried out by him, and always with a strict methodology to be followed and an expectation of absolutely accurate results.

"There were strict rules and, after you'd done your calculations, there were set ways of checking your work. There was an order of doing things. You'd go from the first sheet to the first copy and then the second copy, progressively working your way through the range of numbered copies. Then, when you'd finished, you'd read back over the different versions, checking the last copy against the original and the first copy to make sure they were all the same. And to make absolutely sure everything was correct, a second person would go through your calculations and the rest of your work."

And if a mistake was made?

"If you made even a small mistake—if you were a penny out or a foot out, or even just an inch out—the manager would make you correct the mistake and check it again because he believed that such a mistake might cover a multitude of sins."

However, it was not all work and no play as Colin made the most of his time working in London. In addition to the previously mentioned solo walks in and around central London, there were strolls with a colleague called Cliff Broe.

"He was a quantity surveyor who was about ten years older than me," says Colin, "and we shared an interest in paintings. We'd talk about art, and sometimes we'd walk down to galleries on Charing Cross Road and look at the pictures there."

Another regular lunchtime venue for the friends was the Ministry of Health building close to the LMR offices. Opposite the Freemasons' Hall, just a stone's throw from the entrance to Euston station, the friends were passing the building one day when they discovered its staff restaurant.

"We'd seen this sign that referred to a first-floor restaurant. So even though we didn't work there we thought we'd chance our arm and see if we'd get served. Going in, nobody challenged us and so we had lunch there. Well, not only did we enjoy the food, which was very good, we also enjoyed the low cost, thanks to the vastly reduced staff discount the restaurant offered.

"From then on we went there regularly for probably the best part of a year until, one day in December, we made a big mistake. That particular day they were serving up Christmas lunches, and as we went to get ours we were asked which office we were from.

"We gave them a fictitious room name and number and, as we weren't challenged, we thought we'd got away with it, that we'd called their bluff."

They were wrong. The made-up office details had been easily seen through, and the details of their deception passed back to their boss at LMR.

"Mr Denute called us into his office and gave us a roasting and then, as we left, said with a slight smile on his face, 'You'll have to go somewhere else for lunch now, won't you?'"

And Colin did. One place was called Schmidt's, a German/Austrian restaurant that was just a few hundred yards walk from the LMR office, the Charlotte Street establishment serving up "cracking food", including superb Wiener schnitzel. A nearby Italian restaurant was another lunchtime haunt.

"A tiny place, it was, that I'd go to several days a week," Colin reveals, "and so I came to know the proprietor very well, well enough, in fact, that one day I tried to get him to reveal the recipe of one of the restaurant's best dishes, their spaghetti Bolognaise.

"But he just shook his head and said, 'No!'

"So I tried a different approach, 'Well, how do you get it to be just right?'

"And he looked at me, smiled and pointed at a giant pot in the restaurant kitchen, 'See that big, heavy pot? That is on the stove 24 hours a day, 365 days a year. You just put another ingredient in, stir it and serve it up. And that's how we cook our sauce!'"

In addition to the work, walks and good food that Colin enjoyed during his time in London, Colin also found time to study, spending half a day each week at the Northern Polytechnic in Islington. Having previously determined to qualify as a quantity surveyor, Colin enrolled on a five-year degree course at the polytechnic, but he's honest enough to admit that he made the wrong choice.

"I went to try to achieve a quite difficult surveying qualification. I was really bored by the course, though, so I didn't do that."

Despite quitting the course after just nine months, the time spent at the polytechnic had not been wasted as, many years later, when working with computer systems, knowledge gained on the long-since aborted course would come in useful.

Meanwhile, back home in Bletchley, Colin was by this time going steady with his future wife Norma, whose father, like Colin's, was yet another of the area's railway employees. Norman Lewtas worked as a station foreman.

While Norma lived and worked locally as a secretary at this time, her fiancé continued to commute into London until, in 1955, he left his job with London Midland Railways to take up a new role with a Luton-based building company. Hired as a land surveyor and site development draughtsman by HC Janes, Colin would travel to plots the company had bought, and survey the land on which the company planned to construct houses and factories.

By far the largest building project he worked on in this dual role was one on the northern edge of Luton. Today Bramingham still retains its ancient woodland as well as the original farmstead that gave its name to the area and which, in the mid-1950s, yielded up 800 acres of fields which Colin helped to survey in preparation for the new housing estate his employers would go on to build on the former farmland, which was a greenfield location. One charming and unusual incident vividly shows just how rural the site was back then before the building works were fully underway. Colin chuckles when he explains further.

"It was a completely raw site, just fields and nothing else, and I was out there taking measurements with a colleague, who was the epitome of a sturdy countryman, when, looking around, I shouted out, 'Look! There's a hare over there!'

"My colleague glanced up and, showing no urgency or surprise, simply said, in a matter-of-fact tone of voice, 'Do you want to catch it, boy?'

"I replied excitedly, 'What, me? How on earth would I do that?'

"He replied, 'I'll tell you what to do,'—and proceeded to explain that a hare, being chased, would run around in ever diminishing circles until it became exhausted.

"He set me on the right path and told me to chase the hare but running in shorter circles than the hare to conserve his energy and stamina. After a while the hare, true to form, was exhausted and stood still in the middle of the circle it had created, allowing my colleague to simply walk up to it and catch it. I presume that he had hare pie that evening."

This close encounter is not the only story from around this time to have an animal connection.

The second tale begins with Colin driving along a road on his way to work.

"It was just a normal day and I'm sure I wasn't drunk!" he jokes.

What happened next though was far from normal. Coming up to a junction, a furniture lorry suddenly pulled out and car and lorry collided. Luckily no one sustained any serious injuries but the noise made by the collision brought helpers hurrying to the scene, as Colin explains: "The crash occurred right outside a vet's. Consequently, and in no time at all, a nurse from the surgery appeared to see what had just happened. I'd taken a bang to the head and the gash was bleeding quite a bit. She took one look at me and said, 'Come on, you'd better come inside.'

"The next thing I know I'm in the surgery and I hear the vet saying 'Clear the operating table, please'. Then he laid me out on it and promptly stitched me up!"

Norma and Colin had only been married for a few weeks at this time, with Norma working for Associated Ethyl in Bletchley. Once the company heard about Colin's accident, it immediately collected him from the vet's surgery, took him to Luton Hospital and, after he was patched up, Sydney, the driver, took him back home to their flat in Bletchley.

Colin & Norma on their wedding day

Love & Marriage

Colin was soon back at work after his accident. He was also settling down to married life as on 16 February 1957 Colin Read and Norma Ellen Lewtas had tied the knot, with the bride's home residence listed on the marriage certificate as 47 North Crescent, Fenny Stratford.

The wedding service was conducted by the Reverend Cyril A Wheeler, the vicar at Saint Martin's Church in Aylesbury Street, Fenny Stratford. This church, which had been given listed status just a couple of years earlier, was just a long stone's throw from where Colin had grown up. It was also well known locally as the home of the Fenny Poppers, six small cannon which to this day are fired annually on 11 November, which as well as being Armistice Day is also Saint Martin's Day.

There were no loud booms or bangs to accompany Colin and Norma's wedding, although as the newly-weds were driven away after the ceremony the air was filled with the sound of metal clinking and clanking. This din was caused by the irons that their friends had tied to the car's back bumpers. These irons were from Weatherhead's, a local retailer which sold radios and other electrical goods, and the shop above which the newly-weds were set to make their first home. First, though, there was the little matter of a honeymoon, which began in a first-class carriage of a southbound train heading to London.

As a relatively new member of the HC Janes's staff, Colin had been granted very little time off for his honeymoon, but this didn't stop Mr and Mrs Read, as they now were, from making the most of their two-day break.

First stop on reaching London was the Rembrandt Hotel. Situated then as now in Thurloe Place in Kensington, directly opposite the Victoria and Albert Museum and a short walk from Harrods, the Rembrandt was where the couple spent their wedding night after first dining out at a swish restaurant close to the Comedy Theatre (now the Harold Pinter Theatre).

Once back in Bletchley, and living in their first marital home together, Colin continued to apply his love of woodworking, making new furniture for their flat out of his favourite timber.

"I'd bought these sheets of a special plywood while I was working for LMR in London. I took them with me on the train home, too, which was a bit of an experience! It was worth it, though, because they were beautifully veneered with a hardwood called Meranti. This is an Indonesian mahogany-like timber that I liked so much that we eventually named our first house Meranti."

For the time being, though, the husband and wife team lived in their High Street flat. Outside of work they were both members of a local amateur dramatics group they'd joined in their late teens.

The Bletchco Players had begun life in 1944, the year the British co-operative movement had celebrated its centenary. In Bletchley this was marked by a grand pageant, which in turn gave birth to the drama group.

"We used to have a lovely time," Colin declares. "The players were based in the Co-op building, above the store that was in Albert Street, and we would put on plays and musicals.

Then and now, music also played a big part in Colin's life. A lifelong fan of jazz, Colin joined a small music appreciation society which met at its headquarters in Bletchley Road, Bletchley. From his teen years on he'd take along and play his records of jazz favourites like Ella Fitzgerald and the Ted Heath Band. It was through this appreciation group, too, that his passion for playing music took hold.

A Year of Change

1957 was a watershed year for Colin, and not solely because it began with his marriage to Norma. Still a young man, just 22 years old at the time of his wedding, by year's end he would have switched jobs, taken on a second, part-time role, and hatched plans for building a house to live in. "HC Janes was not a nice company to work for. The job incorporated the land survey skills that I had developed, yet I wanted something more. Surveying was interesting enough and I did a lot of work all over the place with Janes, but I wanted to be a constructor. I wanted to build the buildings. I wanted to get involved in design too. And so I joined Drabble, a company I'd had dealings with while working for HC Janes."

Drabble was a leading local building company in the Bletchley area. Soon after joining the firm, Colin, who was now wearing three hats—surveyor, site engineer and site manager—was taken under the wing of Jimmy Drabble, the son of the company owner.

"He seemed to like me, Jimmy. He was a strange sort of bloke in some ways, but he had plans for the future—he wanted us to build better, more quickly and be better organised. He was also happy to send me on work-study courses.

"Before long I was doing so well that I became a planning officer for the company, working out the construction details for projects. I'd calculate the number of machines a job would need, how much labour would be required and so on. I was also a site officer. Yes, there was a lot to do, but it was like falling off a log to me," he adds.

Second Job Leads to New Home

With more responsibility, and his increased knowledge, came an improved salary, but money for the Reads was still quite tight so Colin took on a second job.

"I got a part-time post working Saturdays for the local estate agent, Charles Neal. I used to go around the area looking for property the company could sell on or could advise people about."

Bringing in much needed additional income, this work also provided an unexpected secondary benefit.

"One day I got a tip-off about some land next to the A5 in Bletchley, quite near the railway line that goes to Bedford. I went to have a look and came across this house, a very big house with a large garden. There were a lot of fir trees there and a tree house, and also what looked like some spare land to the side of the house."

Colin really liked what he'd seen, his mind working overtime on what could be done to develop this prime plot of land. But his plans for the site did not include Charles Neal. Instead, he became determined to buy the land in order to build a home for Norma and himself.

"I used to call Mrs Faulkner, the lady who owned the property, every month for the best part of a year, and when I pressed her about selling, she kept saying, 'Oh, I'll think about it Colin, I'll think about it. I'd like you to have it but I'm not sure I'm ready to sell just yet."

Then one day, when Colin called to see the owner, she'd changed her mind.

"I'm prepared to put it up for sale," she said.

"Well, it'll probably be me who comes to buy it!" Colin replied, gently pressing his case.

"I'll be happy with that," she said, "but what do you want to do with it?"

The explanation that Colin envisaged building a bungalow and selling off part of the land presented no problems. "I'd like you to do it quickly," replied Mrs Faulkner, "so I want £750 for the land."

At this time Colin's weekly wage was less than £20 and, with no savings, he set out to secure a loan to enable him to buy his dream plot.

The first port of call was his local bank in Fenny Stratford. When told the amount Colin wanted to borrow, and the reason why he wanted to borrow such a sum, the bank manager, a Mr Smith, posed a challenging question. "And what collateral have you got, Mr Read?"

"Well, I've got a plot of land."

"No you haven't," said the manager. "You want money to buy the land."

"It's the same thing!" Colin countered.

"And how do you make that out?" the bank manager enquired, raising his eyebrows.

There then followed a discussion which Colin remembers all too well. "He really put me to the test. Looking back, it was my first real sales job, trying to convince this experienced bank manager to lend me £750. At last, though, he said to me, 'Well, I still don't know why I should lend you this money. Can you give me seven good reasons?'

"I can give you one very good reason, Mr Smith," Colin said. "If you don't let me borrow this money, and I don't pay you the interest on the loan, you won't make any money out of me, will you?"

"And do you know what? He laughed, and gave me the £750!"

With his loan secured and the property purchased, the next main tasks were to raise a mortgage and to persuade the council's town planning officers to grant planning permission. Securing a mortgage came relatively easily due to a combination of increased earnings and the sale of half the land Colin had just bought.

"Before long Drabble's started giving me bigger jobs to manage, and so I was soon earning enough to pay the mortgage—I think the whole house project cost me £2,500. On top of that, I cut the one and a half acre plot in two and sold half of it for £500."

The selling and PR skills that had just come to the fore in Colin's bank manager's office were now put to good use and developed during meetings with the lady who'd sold Colin his newly acquired land, and in dealings with the Bletchley town planners, whose blessing he needed before beginning construction of his bungalow on Staple Hall Road, Fenny Stratford.

"I know it sounds corny, but I did everything the lady wanted me to do. Then again, if you're a good salesman you can sell yourself. Plus I was very young and she seemed to like me."

And if there were hitches along the way, Colin tackled them full on and honestly.

"I wouldn't go in and con anybody. That was the last thing I'd do. No, I went through everything with her and made sure she felt comfortable with what was going on."

It was a similar story with the planners, as Colin explains: "I put in for planning permission with some fear and trepidation because there was nothing like my design anywhere in the country at that time."

This design for a three-bedroom bungalow, which Colin describes as "revolutionary", he'd put together from reading articles in trade magazines, the finishing touches being added to the design in July 1958.

"Because of my work, and my interest in architecture, I knew quite a bit about buildings, and so when I came across this idea for a prefab structure that was being used on the Continent, I decided to go with it. Like I say, though, I thought the planners in Bletchley might not give their approval. But in those days the planning process was more personal than it is now, so I talked with them and soon found out that they liked it. In fact, the whole town council became interested afterwards and, when we'd finished construction, everyone on the council was delighted with the bungalow's design."

With planning consent granted, the Reads wasted no time in starting on their building project. Thankfully, there were no major hold-ups, with the new landowners doing much of the construction work, as Colin vividly recalls:

"I put the roof on, laid the floor, made shutters and, as there was no such thing as ready-mixed concrete in those days, I bought in the gravel and sand, borrowed a mixer and got a gang of men to mix the concrete. We were there a couple of days laying the floor, and then we built the rest of the property on top."

Another task was taken on by Colin, Norma and Colin's father. This involved digging a soakaway, which they started one Sunday morning. Walter had just one condition in return for his help: Colin would take him for a midday pint.

"I was okay with that, but when Sunday lunchtime came around Norma decided not to join us. She carried on digging while we went off for a drink. Eventually, when we staggered back from the pub we'd been drinking at, we heard this faint cry—'Colin! Colin! I'm down in this hole.' She'd been digging the soakaway hole while we were gone and she couldn't get out!"

Labour-intensive though it was, and despite having to work on his new-build project while holding down a full-time job, just eight to nine months after building work had begun, Colin and Norma moved into their new home.

On the work front, too, the focus was on house building, with approximately 70 per cent of the properties Drabble's worked on being residential. For Colin, though, much of his time with the company was spent working not on building sites but in the purchasing department.

The house at Bletchley that Colin built

"Salesmen and buyers, there's not much difference, you know, so I did a good job as a buyer. Jimmy was still giving me all the training I'd been promised, but when I wasn't off on courses I'd be in the office getting good deals, going out to possible vendors, looking for the best quotes I could get for, say, 10,000 tiles."

Initially Colin was based in Bletchley but later he transferred to the Drabble office in Cannon Street, Wellingborough. There he continued in his role as a buyer, combining this work with drawing duties, though not quantity surveying. Then he saw a job advertised, an intriguing job, one that Colin believed was made for him.

From Drabble to Winton Hayes to Marriott

At the time this job ad was published, Colin was in his mid-twenties. Married to Norma and living in a stylish three-bedroomed bungalow he had both designed and built, he had benefitted greatly from the personal support of the boss's son and had increased the range of his expertise and his income in the four years he had by then worked for Drabble.

But he wanted more. Specifically, he wanted exactly what the Biggleswade firm of Winton Hayes seemed to be offering. Colin had read the job description for the company's vacant post and was convinced that he was the perfect person to fill the role.

"As far as I was concerned, I was probably the only person that fitted the bill. They wanted a quantity surveyor, site manager, surveyor all rolled into one—and I had it all. I was already doing that job for Drabble's."

Colin's paternal grandparents

Colin's maternal grandmother, Grandmother
Green, with her pet dog Kim, circa 1952

Another football cup for Walter!

Colin in 1939

Colin's mother & father on holiday in Blackpool

Top: Colin, second from left, back row,
with the Scouts in Bletchley, 1951
Bottom: Colin aged 17 with his birds

Top: Colin making furniture in 1957
Bottom: RAF station West Kirby, Colin
middle row, fourth from right

Wedding day

70

Baby Philip at Bletchley

Colin's father Walter holding Philip

Family portrait

a vital material, its effect on the critical path can be seen straight away. Management can then examine what can be done to make up for lost time, either by rearranging the project, or accelerating some of the activities on the critical path. The tendency to 'crash' everything when a project falls behind schedule disappears.

Side effects. In the same way, possession of such accurate control information has enabled Marriott to make the best possible use of manpower, especially in getting the right men to the right job at the right time.

Then there is the effect on suppliers and sub-contractors. Here Brook likes to quote the story of how he phoned the chairman of a major steel supplier and complained that if delivery was not made by a certain date it would seriously delay Marriott's whole building contract. "Well, we got the steel on time," says Brook. "Of course, it's difficult to assess whether it was my roaring over the phone that did the trick or the repeated reference to our computer scheduling. But we have found time and time again with suppliers that CPA does make a difference.

"You see with normal ordering most contractors will deliberately set delivery dates well in advance of their needs. The suppliers know this. But when they know you are using networks and computers and that the delivery times set are accurately calculated so as to complete the job, they generally get the goods to you on time."

These are but a few of the benefits. Brook can list many more. But possibly the best advertisement of all for CPA as far as the firm is concerned is how it has helped Marriott complete contracts ahead of time. The accompanying table speaks for itself.

New project. The next stage for the company in its move into the world of computers is to set up a computer-controlled integrated management system. Brook believes that "this could revolutionise the operation of building firms in that all our knowledge and experience would be housed in a computer memory instead of in books on a shelf."

This project, however, is still very much at the research stage, and is likely to remain this way until the Ministry of Public Building and Works gives a firm lead on what type of computer standardisation it thinks is right. Such a decision from Marriott's point of view cannot come soon enough■

Colin Read: key man behind Marriott's CPA effort

CPA—its effect on contract completions

Breeze Hill School, Wellingborough

(a) Type	...	Secondary School for Girls.
(b) Value	...	£197,692.
(c) Possession of Site	...	December 1, 1965.
(d) Contract Completion Date	...	August 31, 1967.
(e) Actual Completion Date	...	April 3, 1967.
(f) Saving on Contract Period	...	22 weeks.

Wyton Houses

(a) Type	...	Erection of 314 Officers' and Airmen's Houses with 113 garages, etc.
(b) Value	...	£976,503 6s 10d.
(c) Possession of Site	...	March 1, 1965.
(d) Contract Completion Date	...	February 28, 1967.
(e) Actual Completion Date	...	December 7, 1966.
(f) Saving on Contract Period	...	17 weeks.

Lakenheath Houses

(a) Type	...	Erection of 408 American Airmen's Houses.
(b) Value	...	£1,447,404 18s. 2d.
(c) Possession of Site	...	April 14, 1964.
(d) Contract Completion Date	...	April 14, 1966. Actual construction time, 21 months.
(e) Actual Completion Date	...	January 14, 1966.
(f) Saving on Contract Period	...	12 weeks.

Barby School

(a) Type	...	Primary School.
(b) Value	...	£28,949 16s. 10d.
(c) Possession of Site	...	April 10, 1967
(d) Contract Completion Date	...	October 2, 1967.
(e) Actual Completion Date	...	September 4, 1967.
(f) Saving on Contract Period	...	4 weeks.

Horatio Myer Limited

(a) Type	...	Extensions to Factory.
(b) Value	...	£106,760 13s. 4d.
(c) Possession of Site	...	June 1, 1966.
(d) Contract Completion Date	...	April 1, 1967.
(e) Actual Completion Date	...	March 7, 1967.
(f) Saving on Contract Period	...	3 weeks.

Wellingborough Girls' High School

(a) Type	...	Extensions to Girls' High School.
(b) Value	...	£151,699 18. 10d.
(c) Possession of Site	...	June 1, 1966.
(d) Contract Completion Date	...	August 31, 1967.
(e) Actual Completion Date	...	July 27, 1967.
(f) Saving on Contract Period	...	5 weeks.

Colin, pictured in *Building Industry Week*, November 1967

After applying and securing his dream job, Colin's future seemed bright. The reality, however, proved to be anything but, and just a year after joining his new employer he quit. HC Janes had been a "professional" outfit, Drabble's had "taught me a lot", but Colin's verdict on Winton Hayes is unequivocal and scathing:

"They were an awful firm," he declares. "It was a good job for me to have, and in some ways I learned a lot doing it, but the company was just so backward! I made money for the company and I reorganised their building operations, and the bosses were happy enough, but I soon realised that I'd need to find somewhere else to work because the job didn't stretch me. In fact, the stuff I was doing for Winton Hayes bored me."

That said, there was more to his decision to move than personal dissatisfaction, there was the broader picture, the far-reaching, industry-wide changes that were in the air, changes Colin was well aware of and wanted to embrace and help bring about.

"I'd read a lot, and because of this I knew about things others didn't and which they could never have dreamed of. Contractors, especially, they just went about putting up buildings in the same old way and hoped for the best!"

For Colin, though, he'd seen the blueprint for the future and it had a decidedly Continental look to it. "In Europe they were years ahead of us when it came to construction work, and I knew their methods were the way forward. For example, there was evidence to show that a company should commit to building not more than 250 houses, yet in this country firms were still taking on government contracts to put up 750 properties, and going to the wall in the process. So I could see that the building industry needed to do things in a very different way to companies like Winton Hayes. I think I was right, too, because the year after I left them, the firm went bust."

During the short period spanning 1962 to 1963, however, it was not just radical changes within the building industry that were having a profound effect on Colin. At home, the Reads' lives were transformed by the birth of their first child, the proud parents welcoming Philip Ashley into the world on 22 July 1963. In January that year, Colin had moved from Winton Hayes to Robert Marriott Limited. Then, just a few weeks later, the young family of three left Bletchley, and their bungalow home there, to move north to the Bedfordshire village of Podington.

The Very Influential Mr Eric Brook

Founded by Robert Marriott in 1890, the building company Colin joined as chief planning officer and work-study engineer was a well-established firm still run by the Marriott family. One of the founder's sons, Colonel JR Marriott, was the executive chairman, while two other Marriott men served on the firm's board of directors.

With Marriott's strong roots in the past, you could be forgiven for thinking that this Rushden based company might have been a traditionalist, even stuck-in-the-mud outfit, but when Colin wrote to Marriott offering them his services, he knew this was absolutely not the case.

"The company had a very good reputation for building quality housing. More than that, though, they had a reputation as one of the best-organised middle-sized companies in the building industry, and so I wrote to tell them I was interested in finding a job that would stretch my imagination. I didn't apply for an advertised job, though. I made up the role I wanted to carry out. They liked what I wrote, offered me an interview and then offered me a job."

When working for Drabble, Colin had been taken under the wing of Jimmy Drabble. Within a short time of linking up with Marriott, another senior manager had taken a shine to him. He was a man who would have a major and lasting impact not just on what Colin did in his working life, but also on how and why he did what he did. This man was the company's managing director, Eric A Brook.

A heavy smoker and a man who liked a drink or two, Brook was a tall and slim man, maybe 55 to 60 years old. He was also a successful boss, who drove a Rolls-Royce, and a driven character, a manager who combined a no-nonsense approach with an innovative and inspirational leadership style. From the outset Brook impressed Colin, although initially this respect was mixed with trepidation.

"I stood to attention when he came into the room," Colin says, only half-joking, "and I always called him Mr Brook. We were never close, but he treated me with a great deal of respect and I treated him the same."

Despite this rather cool relationship, the master and his apprentice were good for each other and good for Marriott. So good, in fact, that Colin believes Eric Brook to be the "best businessperson" he's ever met, read about or seen on television.

"He would comprehend exactly what you were doing. You'd walk into his office to see him about something, some job or other, and there was no small talk, it was just straight down to business. And he'd have two sheets of paper on his desk with all the details of the projects I'd be working on. It wasn't just what he did and what he knew either, it was the keenness and the interest he showed, which we all came to share."

An example of Brook's infectious man management skills was evident in one of Colin's first meetings with his boss. "I wanted to talk to him because I felt uncomfortable doing something on one of our projects."

Eventually summoning up the courage to approach Mr Brook, Colin turned up for his meeting at the agreed time, knocked on the MD's door and entered his office.

"Come in, Colin, and sit down," said his boss before immediately getting to the heart of his new young employee's concerns.

"I'm sorry I haven't had time to speak to you enough about this job. You seem to be troubled about the time these people are taking to make these parts."

He then went on to explain the solution he'd lined up.

"I've had a word with a friend of mine," he revealed. "He's retired now, Fred Jones, but I've asked him if he'll spend some time with you to help you get through this particular job. Is that all right with you?"

Colin just nodded and said yes.

Other meetings impressed upon the younger man the importance of preparing properly. A shrewd operator when it came to lodging winning tenders for work, Mr Brook would call his planners in on the weekend if there was a possibility that a contract could be won by doing so.

"Quotes back then had to be tendered by noon on Mondays, and so Mr Brook, in his wisdom, decided that putting our quote in at the last minute gave us a better chance of finding out what rival companies were including in their bid documents. As a result, we'd sometimes be called in on a Saturday or Sunday morning for planning meetings. I must have attended a dozen or more of these."

The first of several projects Eric Brook would hand Colin the responsibility for was a work study concerning the company's joinery works.

"We employed 20-odd people in the joinery section, making windows and doors and so on," says Colin. "To cut a long story short, I had to examine every procedure. I spent a year doing that, looking at every detail, even small details that would ensure, for example, that a man would handle a piece of wood once, not twice; that workers' time was used efficiently and effectively; and, of course, that everything that took place did so in the right order and on time."

Presenting Brook with his report, Colin was pleased to find that both his boss and the joinery manager accepted his findings, "My report stated that if my findings were implemented, the joinery works would carry out x per cent more work and would be 25 per cent more profitable for Marriott."

The joinery workers had been concerned that they would suffer if the proposals made by Colin in his work-study report were rolled out. "They were worried that if Eric Brook acted on my report, they'd have their wages cut, and they would've been if I hadn't been good at what I did. But in the end they were better off and some of the staff even came to see me and they said, 'You know, you were right, Colin.'"

There was one dissenting voice, however.

"Everybody in the firm seemed to like my plan. Everyone, that is, except Colonel Marriott, whom I ran into in a corridor one afternoon just after I'd presented my report to Eric Brook. He looked at me and said, 'I say, Colin Read, isn't it?'

"'Yes, Colonel,' I replied

"'Just tell me, how the devil do you get 25 per cent profit from this scheme of yours?'

"My answer was, 'I worked it out, sir.'

"Well, he just said 'Huh!' and walked off without another word."

Despite this scepticism, Colin's stock continued to rise, with the result that he was increasingly taken into the managing director's confidence, soon becoming Eric Brook's right-hand man.

As Colin puts it, "He was my manager and I was his personal assistant, and because of this he kept on putting more work my way, as well as encouraging me to go on courses. I was taken to Europe by him, too. We went to Brussels to see the European Parliament building being constructed. I also accompanied Mr Brook to a meeting with two British Government officials, and I ended up doing all the drawing and all the costings for various bids.

"After we were awarded a contract by the Government, I was given one contract after another to work on."

The 1960s in Britain was the decade of the high-rise with many new residential and office tower blocks rising up above urban streets.

Marriott bucked this trend, concentrating mostly on two-storey housing. Colin's favourite project during this period, however, was neither a high-rise tower nor another mass-housing build, but an altogether more unusual one that geographically would take him out to the Cotswolds and, work wise, into uncharted territory.

The setting for this project was a former RAF base at Moreton-in-Marsh which, in 1959, had been bought by the fire service. Seven years later the 500-acre site officially became the home of the new Fire Service Technical College, this change of use formally revealed by the then home secretary Roy Jenkins, a man who, during World War II, had spent time working a few hundred yards from the Read family home as a code breaker at Bletchley Park.

With responsibility for transforming the ex-RAF base falling to Robert Marriott Limited, the company devoted two years to working on a project that, for Colin, proved to be an eye-opening experience.

"We won the contract to build the college, and I can honestly say I've never been involved in anything like it before or since."

The old RAF Nissen huts were left intact—these would stay in use as dormitories—but the new specialist training buildings were set to be purpose-built constructions that would be put to unconventional use as modern training facilities, as Colin reveals:

"We had to make buildings that would look and function like real buildings, but also be buildings that could be set alight day after day."

For Colin, this was a fascinating job to be working on, especially as he had been given more control over aspects of this project than he had been allowed on any previous one. It also meant that he faced unusual challenges, most notably replicating boats, aeroplanes, houses and tower-blocks using reinforced concrete.

Also different was the proportion of the project given over to installing services such as electricity and water. On a regular, everyday construction project the services' budget would have been approximately 25 per cent of the overall spend, but here it was 75 per cent.

"I was liaising with the tradesmen, getting people together. It was difficult making sure, for example, that plumbers and electricians agreed to proceed in a proper manner. But we met all our construction targets, and we made a profit too."

While the Moreton-in-Marsh project focused on converting a former RAF base, the project that saw Marriott managers pitch up at another site at the far end of Cornwall saw minds turn to modifying a working air-force site. Just as challenging in its own way as the Fire Service Training Centre, the contract at Culdrose didn't get past the tendering stage.

"It was the windiest and wettest place, which was used as an air-sea rescue unit," says Colin. "The RAF wanted to build new accommodation for the staff that worked there, so I went to survey the site."

He researched the site and the prospective job thoroughly and, when drafting plans and budgets, took into account the inclement weather that would likely affect building works, but in his final report he concluded that he couldn't see how Marriott could do the job the RAF wanted the company to deliver. Eric Brook then set to work building into the company's tender what Colin calls his "magic figures". Sadly, despite his wizardry, the contract was awarded to another bidder.

Farewell Fenny Stratford, Hello Podington

While his work in the 1960s led to Colin travelling far and wide, it was one short journey early in that decade that was to have the longest-lasting impact on the lives of Colin and Norma.

They made this journey one winter's day in late 1962, a drive that led them to a little village tucked away in the countryside roughly halfway between Wellingborough and Bedford.

Having patiently bided their time waiting for the sale of the land that had eventually become the site of their ultra-modern bungalow, gone through the planning application hoops, then put long hours into constructing their dream home, after living in The Beeches for just four years, the Reads drove to Podington in their search for a new home. What had brought about this sudden change of direction? The reason, according to Colin, was simple:

"We were young and ambitious and, at that time, I really wanted to work for Marriott. Then, when I got a job with them, I knew I'd feel more comfortable living close to Rushden, where the company was based. We looked at various places within about five miles of Rushden, but when we visited Podington we both really liked it and its country nature."

A picturesque place that is mentioned in the Domesday Book, Podington is located right up in the north-west corner of Bedfordshire a few miles from Rushden, and it was here that the Reads came across a house for sale. This house in the village, with a population of just a few hundred, would soon become home to Colin, Norma and baby son, Philip.

"It was a dormer bungalow with two bedrooms and a bathroom upstairs," Colin reveals. "Downstairs was another bedroom and an en-suite bathroom, a kitchen, hallway and study-cum-dining room. Outside we had a half-acre back garden. It was a nice house, even though it needed lots of remedial work doing. We had plenty of fun there."

Having sold their Fenny Stratford home, they moved into the Podington property in February 1963, a month when the village, just like everywhere else in the UK, was still enduring the record-breaking cold spell and wintry snowfalls that paralysed the country for weeks on end.

"I couldn't get into work. In fact, we couldn't get anywhere much. And on two days, when we were snowed in, the family went out sledging on the slopes around the village. I can even remember sledging about 100 yards down one particular hill. It was a lot of fun, and I think that the snowy conditions then brought the community together.

We certainly got to know the community, and it got to know us too."

At that time, Podington still had a butcher and a baker, a couple of pubs, a club and a post office. It was also home to Margaret Smith and her doctor husband, David, a man who would later come to Norma's aid when she went into labour prior to giving birth to second son, Jonathan.

"We'd moved into one of the few local houses to have been built in the post-war period. The village was very close knit and small, and there'd been very little development and few new residents either. So it didn't take long before we met the Smiths. In fact, our paths crossed on our first day in the village, and just two days later we went round to dinner at their house in Gold Street. We became firm friends, and I ended up designing and fitting a new kitchen in the Smiths's home," says Colin.

As well as Dr and Mrs Smith, and other new found Podington friends, Colin and Norma continued to meet up with the old crowd from their Bletchley days, a social group that included Colin's sister and her partner, Peter. On leaving school, Susan had become an air hostess with the giant airline company BOAC, her job taking her on regular transatlantic trips, one of which ended with Peter losing his job, as Colin explains:

"Susan was flying back from one of her trips to America. She'd go for three or four weeks at a time and would come back with cases and bags, so on this occasion Peter decided to meet her at the airport. He was with Aston Martin in Newport Pagnell at the time and had a really good job with them as a regional sales manager.

"Anyway, at this particular time, a rich Arab sheik was getting his Aston Martin serviced—spending more on it, by the way, than I'd spend on buying a car!—and after the work had been done, Peter was asked by one of the directors to take the car on a test run to make sure everything was fine before the owner came to collect it.

"Well, Peter wasn't satisfied with just driving it around the block and back. Instead, he decides to go and meet Susan in the sheik's Aston Martin. So off he drives in this smart and shiny luxury car and, Peter being Peter, he manages to pull rank and drive the car right up to the gateway that the BOAC aircrew were due to pass through after landing."

So far so good. Unfortunately, though, the plan then came completely unstuck. By a huge coincidence, the owner of the car happened to be there too. Reporting this to the director of the company, the upshot was that Peter was fired by Aston Martin.

This isn't the only car-related story Colin tells concerning the motor-mad man who became his brother-in-law. "One night, the four of us—Susan, Peter, Norma and me—had been out together and we were making our way home in our separate cars. We were following Peter and Susan in a little old thing we owned, while he was racing off ahead in yet another car. Then, as he went to turn a corner, he tipped the car over. Luckily, though, Susan got out without even a scratch on her but Peter's head was badly cut. Luckily, there was a St John Ambulance man living nearby who treated him."

This accident didn't go down at all well with Susan and Colin's mother, who at that time saw Peter as "a lot of trouble". However, despite her reservations, the relationship flourished, with the couple later marrying and setting up home in Bloxham near Banbury. The marriage proved highly successful, too, the pair going on to have three children.

Meanwhile, back in the Reads' new family home in Podington, Norma started up her own business, Read Typing Service, which subsequently become Alpha Duplicating, printing publications such as *The American Car Magazine* and *Higham Ferrers Newsletter* on a machine installed in the garage. Much of the business was sourced by Colin.

Round Tabler Read

Socially, too, the Reads were spreading their wings in their new community. Colin took on the role of bar secretary for the village cricket club, and he was also heavily involved with the Round Table organisation.

"I became a member in September 1962, just before we left the Bletchley area. Round Tables in those days were very sociable men's organisations, and it was an honour to be asked to join. I thought it sounded like a very good thing to be involved in, helping to raise money for good causes and having a good time socially.

"Two men put me forward for membership. One was my GP, Dr Murphy. I was pretty good friends with his son. He proposed me while, oddly, the man who seconded my membership proposal was Michael Ramsbottom, a Bletchley man who'd owned the nursery that was alongside my home when I was a child. And that was the same nursery, of course, that we'd scrumped apples in when my friends and I were boys!"

As things turned out, Colin had been a Round Tabler in his home town for just a few months when he and Norma (and baby Philip) upped sticks and moved to Podington. As a result, the Bletchley RT approached the branch secretary of the Rushden branch to arrange a transfer, which effectively occurred on 31 December 1962.

"We went along to the Rushden Round Table's New Year's Eve party, which was held at a place in Shirley Road called the Westward Hotel, which was run by a Round Table man called Peter Neville. I was introduced to the members, had a great night and soon afterwards became an official Rushden RT member.

"After that, I gradually took on more and more tasks and was involved with putting on all sorts of activities.

"Our goal was to make as much money as we could from our events at little or no cost. One of the most prestigious was the annual air show at Sywell Aerodrome in Northamptonshire. We also put on donkey derbies in the grounds of the Rushden ski club and things like that, but one of the best days out I had was at the Huntingdon Regatta. This was a huge event. It took over two or three fields for car parking and had a beer tent," Colin recalls.

As for his memories of the regatta itself, what he remembers most clearly were the activities that "usually involved people falling in the water". Not that this was the only time watery accidents and incidents have taken place in his long life. In fact, Colin has a treasure trove of boating adventures and misadventures stretching back to one that unfolded on the first warm summer Sunday of 1963.

"A local doctor, Brian Brook, a serious bloke who knew that I'd got a bit of sailing experience, asked me to join him in a boat race at Thrapston sailing lake over the border in Northants, and I agreed to crew for him."

The craft the men were due to race in was a two-man Enterprise dinghy, a four-metre long sloop with brilliant blue sails, sails which Colin would come to see at very close quarters…

"When we got to the lake, Brian, who was a nimble little lad, immediately hopped on-board our dinghy followed straightaway by me, this great big six-foot chap. Well, as soon as I stepped on-board I grabbed the mast and promptly capsized the boat! Brian managed to scramble up on to the side of the dinghy, but I was underneath the mainsail, and so I shouted out, 'I'm all right, Brian!'"

Good news for Colin but less so for the doctor, whose response was, "It's not you, it's the boat I'm worried about!"

Another boating excursion occurred during the 1968 to 1969 season of Round Table events and was described simply in that year's club directory as *Boat Trip, Phipps Brewery Barge*. It was another memorable one for the man listed in the directory as *Colin Read, work study engineer, age 32*, who this time managed to stay out of the water.

"Yes, that was a good trip that was. Phipps Brewery was in Northampton, and we set out by boat from near Milton Keynes, cruising up from there to Northampton."

As one would expect, the party enjoyed a few Phipps beers along the way, even though the company had ceased brewing its renowned draught beer just a few months earlier. Six years later the brewery was no more, although, as Colin points out, in 2014 the resurrected Phipps Company would revive brewing operations at the Albion Street brewery in Northampton.

Around the same time as the brewery excursion, Rushden Round Tablers competed for the Kilpur Trophy, an event which had unlikely origins.

"Two of our members were up in London one time, and while they were there they happened to look in a shop window and see this trophy on display. One of them said to the other, 'What a funny looking trophy that is!'

"And the second one replied, 'Yes, but how about taking it back with us?'

"So they ended up buying it."

Once the trophy was back in Northamptonshire, the two men arranged a series of games—skittles, table tennis and so on—pitting members against a team of former Round Tablers, the winners claiming the trophy, which had been renamed by merging the first three letters of the pair's surnames, Kilsby and Purvis.

Thanks to the regular and wide-ranging events they put on, Colin and fellow members of the Rushden Round Table (number 262) raked in plenty of cash during the dozen or so years he was involved, his own commitment to the cause taking up many non-working hours.

"I reckon I did something or other six days a week during my time as a Round Tabler and put on my dinner jacket to attend a function at least once a week, so about 20 hours a week all told.

"Our branch covered a large geographical area, from Rushden in the west to Whittlesey and Wisbech in the east, and from Stamford southwards to Bedford, and we raised thousands of pounds from our events and allocated the money we raised in different ways, giving grants to various people who applied. For instance, we gave quite a lot of money to the Macmillan organisation, local hospices and so on."

One of the many Round Table hats Colin wore during his time working on their behalf was that of area extension officer. This oddly titled role saw him help set up new branches in neighbouring areas, organising recruitment fairs, arranging promotions and sorting out formal registration details.

"Basically, I was the area representative that made sure things were done in the proper manner according to the Round Table's rules and traditions."

One of the new branches Colin brought into existence in this role was the Sandy and District branch, which, as it happened, became the 1,000th RT branch. To recognise this milestone, Colin and his fellow organisers arranged an induction ceremony for the new set-up, with 1,000 male guests invited to a grand party.

This was staged at Wicksteed Park in Kettering, the second oldest theme park in Britain with its slogan *The Place Where Fun Was Invented*. And on the night Colin's fellow Round Tablers came to visit, fun was most definitely had.

"With so many young men all out for a good night, it wasn't surprising that things got a bit out of hand," he says. "The fun started when someone tied his white napkin to the person next to him, who then tied his to the man sitting next to him, and so it went on. Before we knew it, we had everyone in the place tied together with napkins."

As the evening progressed, and the high spirits of some of the guests rose higher still, so the alcohol-fuelled japes continued.

"At that time Wicksteed Park had some builders in doing some work, and they'd left their equipment, tools and whatnot, outside. Anyway—and this was nothing to do with me—all of a sudden some of the guests appear in the hall where we were all gathered for dinner, carrying 60-foot long pole ladders. There were about ten of these lying around outside, and these blokes brought three of them into the hall and started passing them over our heads. But then, when they went to put them back, they had a real job getting them out again and ended up causing a lot of damage. So I got an ear-bashing from the people who run Wicksteed and had to arrange for compensation to be paid to repair the damage that had been caused."

Panto in Podington

Meanwhile, away from the all-male confines of the Round Table world, and echoing their previous involvement with the Bletchco Players, Colin and Norma became key characters in the creation of what became Podington's annual pantomime. Colin organised these shows, which were put on at the village cricket club where he was bar secretary, with Norma writing the scripts. They both performed in these capers, too. Other regular actors included Tony Norman, who was the manager of a building company; Malcolm Tobin, a shoe man in Rushden;

Alan Addinall, a salesman; and Lee Chambers, a local landscape contractor. Others who trod the boards were John Marriott, a farmer, who belonged to the same family that owned Robert Marriott Limited, John Saxby, Richard Gilbert, Michael Taylor, Barry Hall, Rodney Wildman and Jim Stewart.

As for the origins of the village pantomime, these lay in a joint request that was put to the cricket club one year by the village committee and school.

"They came to us and asked us if we could donate some money to provide presents for Father Christmas to give out at that year's Christmas children's party, but I told the committee that we didn't have enough money in the kitty. Then, when the request was discussed by a group of us at the club, someone said, 'So what can we do?'"

Colin has no idea where the inspiration came from for what he said next, but say it he did.

"Why don't we put on some entertainment ourselves?"

"What do you suggest we do?" someone else replied.

"Mother Goose," exclaimed Colin. "We can just do the whole thing between us."

The group decided to give it a go, and that December they took part in their pantomime premiere with a performance that was short on script but long on improvisation.

"We didn't really have a script. We just ad-libbed our way through, just larking about really, but it brought the house down! Norma was watching, and she enjoyed it so much she said we should have a proper script."

So began a regular event in the Podington social calendar, one the Reads would put on for the next six or seven years with Norma as scriptwriter and Colin one of the regular, all-male cast.

"There were about eight of us who took part and, of course, Norma knew everyone really well, so everything she'd write would relate to the actual performers.

"I don't know why, but I always seemed to end up being a dame or a fairy or something like that!" Colin adds.

Each year the troupe put on two performances. The afternoon one for the village children was staged at Manor Farm, a large house in the village, with the evening performance being put on at the cricket club.

Playing pantomime dames and fairies was not the only performing Colin did back then. He also played drums as a member of the Dominoes Rhythm Group. Drumming had become a passion that had flowered during the years Norma and Colin were living in their Bletchley bungalow, which as well as being the first home they'd owned was a place to play music with friends one day a week.

"A group of us met up at our house every Friday night. One friend played the saxophone, another the trombone, while Norma played the clarinet. There was a trumpet player, too, a good musician who'd taught at Kneller Hall, the Royal Military School of Music's place in Richmond. I played the drums."

Although playing mostly for their own enjoyment, eventually the music-making friends started performing in public, playing what Colin jokingly refers to as "a repertoire of three pieces".

"There was a country pub about halfway between Bletchley and Maids Moreton. It's now a very large dining-pub, but back then we used to go and drink there. We got to know the landlord quite well, and one thing led to another and we ended up in a corner of the pub playing to the customers. However, when the landlord realised we had taken up the room of two dining tables, and he was missing out on dining revenue, he promptly organised for us to play in the village hall instead. We still had a great night!"

Later that summer this band of friends went on the road, to Cambridge. Taking up residency on the banks of the River Cam one afternoon (Norma eight months pregnant), they took out their instruments and launched into one of their favourite numbers.

"What else could we play there but *Down by the Riverside?* That was one of our signature tunes, and it went down well with most people who were there though not the police, unfortunately, who turfed us off our patch!"

A few years on and living in Podington, Colin and some friends in the village then formed the Dominoes Rhythm Group. Dougie George played piano, Steve Bryan, a pig-farm worker by day, was on tea chest bass (home-made by Colin!), while Colin was the drummer. A traditional jazz ensemble, the trio entertained locals in the cricket club bar most Friday evenings.

"The idea for the group came about when Dougie and I were having a chat one day. He'd worked in the shoe trade but was retired by then, and he and I got talking about starting up a little village group. And before we knew it, the idea had taken off."

With Dougie George leading the way, each week the Dominoes Rhythm Group would work its way through a selection of swing and traditional jazz standards to a large and enthusiastic audience.

"The cricket club was probably only big enough to hold about 60 or 70 people, but more than that would turn up. In fact, one evening there were so many people in the place that I thought the walls were going to collapse and the roof cave in!"

The Friday night gigs, which went on so late that they sometimes attracted the attention of the local police, soon became a mainstay of village life, with the Dominoes' musicians enjoying free beer as payment for their passionate musical efforts.

Unsurprisingly, Colin had yet another finger in yet another village event: the annual sports day. This consisted of numerous races involving a cross section of the community, including the whole Read family.

"John Marriott and I would take part in the wheelbarrow race, which took place on the village roads. We used to race down to a crossroads about a mile out of Podington and then race back again. Absolutely knackering it was!"

Village life was different then to how it is now, though, so closing the roads to traffic was no big deal.

"We used to have a word with the village policeman, who lived in Podington, buy him a drink and he'd make sure barriers were put up until the races were done."

All in all, then, life for Colin in the 1960s was a non-stop mix of work, play and, of course, home life.

A second son, Jonathan, completed the Read family on 6 October 1965. Meanwhile, the printing business continued. As well as caring for two young children, Norma used to work at night—sometimes through the night.

A Brave New Building World

Working for a successful, progressive building company led by its dynamic and inspirational MD, Eric Brook, Colin's time at Robert Marriott saw him embrace and utilise the best of modern construction methods. His job title may have been chief planning officer/work-study engineer, but the reality was, that as Brook's protégé, he was whatever his boss wanted him to be—private consultant, chief works engineer, senior planning officer and much more besides. And in his multifaceted role he had continued to introduce productive, modernising changes both large and small.

"In those days most building work in this country was done haphazardly with all the trades subcontracted in. And there was no real co-ordination of these subcontractors. You'd have plumbers in one Wednesday and carpenters in the next. I didn't originate the type of changes that were necessary, but I did make Marriott building sites operate on what was known as 'the line of balance' which meant overlapping the various trades by about a couple of days. This meant less time taken on a site, which in turn saved a lot of money. I also did critical path analysis, or CPA as it was known for short."

At the time Colin linked up with Marriott, it was a medium-sized building firm working on projects in the £100,000–£2m price bracket. His arrival also coincided with the company's first experience of CPA, which it had used on a school-building project in conjunction with the Building Research Establishment in Watford. Already utilised by larger building companies like Laing and Costain, the Marriott model of CPA—which combined drawn-up and computerised networks of critical activities before and during a building project—was fully exploited and overseen by Colin.

The company's use of this CPA tool proved so effective that Marriott's resulting successes caught the attention of the magazine *British Industry Week,* which, in November 1967, ran a feature on the firm with the strapline *You don't have to be big to use modern business methods.* The article detailed how critical path analysis had become central to its management methodology, quoting Colin on how the CPA-led approach was becoming more and more popular with contract managers. The piece also revealed that Colin and his colleagues were planning and managing the company's building projects so well that contract after contract was being finished weeks ahead of the agreed completion date.

Put simply, these impressive, part-computerised results were gained by introducing order and process into operations that had not previously been well ordered or properly processed. On a practical level, one simple, innovative example of a process improvement came out of Colin's understanding of how Continental constructors were running building projects and sites.

"How did you get tiles on to the roof of a house in those days?" asks Colin before answering his own question. "You used what you'd always used: a hod carrier, a man who'd climb up a ladder carrying a hod of tiles for the tilers to lay. But I'd seen what was going on in France and Germany, and so what I decided to do was put in a little mechanical lift, a small hoisting unit. No more men climbing up and down ladders all day, just the tilers up above and, on the ground below, a guy feeding the tiles on to the lift that took the tiles to the blokes up on the roof."

As well as these practical by-products of Colin's research into management techniques, and his implementation of concisely planned and precisely costed projects, there were lecturing offers that came his way from across the country. As a result, he made presentations at National Federation of Builders' conferences in various towns and cities, including Blackpool, Nottingham and Loughborough. The audiences could be challenging as, at that time, builders "didn't want to know anything about computers". Nonetheless, Colin stuck to his guns as he spread the word, and his belief in a computerised future was rewarded with more offers that he was only too pleased to accept.

"I was selected to represent the industry on government committees that had been set up to develop and improve techniques in the building industry," he explains. "And several magazines asked me to write various feature pieces, which I did."

Serving on these government committees, his focus was on nomenclature, effectively drafting standardised and, more importantly, computerised processes for building companies, their suppliers and customers.

"We were trying to put in place standard ways of describing things. To give a very simplified example, a paving slab has three measurements: length, breadth and depth.

At the time we were working on these committees, the industry had no standard formats for describing materials, so what we were doing was establishing a rigid order that would mean the slab's dimensions would always be described length first, then breadth and lastly depth."

Drummer Read Learns to Blow his own Trumpet

Although the seeds of Colin's much-used motto 'Good enough isn't!' had long since sprouted as his career in construction took off, first at Drabble's but especially with Robert Marriott, it was while working for the latter that he learned another valuable and unforgettable lesson.

Sent on a course at nearby Cranfield University, there he met a man called Tom Gardiner.

"I went there on a time-lapse photography course, to learn how to use this kind of photography in the workplace, so that you could set a camera up and leave it to photo images instead of losing time waiting around between shots. In other words, by using time-lapse photography you could now do two things at once. Tom was running this course and I got to like him, and he took a shine to me."

But while this friendship lasted no longer than the duration of the photography course, something Tom Gardiner said one day has remained with him.

"I'd spent a lot of time using computers in my construction work, of course, and I got talking to Tom about this when he suddenly said, 'You've obviously done some good things, Colin, but you won't benefit unless you tell people about them.'"

And on hearing this a penny dropped—and stayed dropped. Or to paraphrase Colin's own motto, he came to realise that 'Good enough isn't—you've also got to show people what you've done'.

"I was showing a bit of promise, but as Tom pointed out I had to do more and, if necessary, I had to get people to adapt and to adopt the principles I believed in."

In practical terms, his record for introducing better working practices at Robert Marriott had been good but, his eyes and ears opened by Gardiner's motivational talk, it wasn't long before his ambition led Colin into a new role that would soon see him putting his photography tutor's advice into practice.

In a nutshell, his work, research and lectures had taught Colin that he was ahead of the game. He saw that major changes were coming as the sun rose at the dawn of the computer age. So, when he was headhunted by Capital Cities Computer Services (CCCS), a Watford-based offshoot of the giant Holst company, he seized the chance to join the revolution.

A Salesman is Born

Colin had been good for Robert Marriott, and working for the company had been good for Colin. Even so, there came a point, in 1969, by which time he was 33 years old, when the itch to leave could no longer be scratched. "I had no real reason to want to leave Marriott. Eric Brook was a good boss and, as well as the responsibility I had for running projects, I was also drafting tutorials about construction and techniques for an international correspondence course and had just been seconded on to a governmental body. I was really doing all right. I'd got a company car—and not many staff at Marriott had one of those—and I was accorded some respect thanks, in part, to the training courses I was putting on.

"When I told Mr Brook I was leaving, he was disappointed. He said he could understand what I'd just told him about the changes that were on the horizon, but he reckoned I was making a mistake."

At the heart of the new role, as initially outlined, was the task of designing and installing computer systems for the benefit of construction companies.

"Because I'd done such a good job at Marriott, Brian Mustoe, the managing director of CCCS, really wanted me to join him and to get this new type of business for his company. He sold me on the idea and offered me £1,000 a year more than I'd been earning and a better car. So I took the job."

As flamboyant as he was persuasive, Mustoe was a Round Table man, which meant that the pair had already met several times before Colin joined CCCS. In the social whirl of Round Table activity, their get-togethers then had been light-hearted and amiable, but a few weeks into Colin's new role—and with the building industry in recession—the mood was altogether different, much more serious, when the two men met up in Brian Mustoe's office.

And, from the first, the gloves were off. "I'd asked for this meeting to establish if I had a job." This is Colin's blunt summary of just why this face to face encounter came to be arranged.

"I said to Brian that I felt he'd got me to join Capital Cities on false pretences, that I'd been expecting the firm's salesmen to be coming to me, saying 'We've got Mr Brown, the builder from down the road, and he wants to do this, that and the other. Can you help him?'. But this hadn't been happening at all. I'd got my office, desk and so on, but I wasn't getting any work."

Mustoe's response was short and to the point.

"Go and get it yourself!"

"I can't do that. I'm not a salesman," replied Colin.

It was then that managing director Mustoe lit the touchpaper. He thrust out his hands, palms upturned, and exclaimed, *"You are!* You're one of the best salesmen I know. How do you think you got on so well at Marriott?" he asked. "Everything you did and did well there involved you selling ideas to people—and they bought them!"

And so, just as Tom Gardiner had recently pointed out to Colin the importance of telling people all about your good work, not hiding your light beneath a bushel, now here was Brian Mustoe spelling it out to him that he was a salesman, an exceptional salesman. For Colin this was another revelation, a pivotal moment in his career as, convinced of his selling abilities by his boss, he set about making his mark in his new regional salesman role.

"When Brian Mustoe told me he thought I was a good salesman, that was the first time anybody had ever said that to me. It was quite releasing. I felt invigorated, and so I became a salesman—and a bloody good one at that!"

Despite Colin's new found zeal and enthusiasm, it was not all plain sailing.

"There was a fair bit of cold calling, and early on that could be awkward," he says, "but I began to find ways in. Every opening I explored, I felt there was something there to go for."

With computer systems still in their infancy in the construction industry, a key aspect of this sales work was finding the right contact to talk to about the benefits to be had from buying Capital Cities' bespoke payroll, sales ledger and stock-control systems, its batch processing options, or the potential to run business and planning applications through the firm's mainframe computer. With a recession biting, though, the building trade market was shrinking fast, and sales had to be sourced in other industries.

This Colin did and, following two highly successful years during which he "took anything on", he was promoted to the post of regional sales manager.

Several 'Jars' & a Lost Car

As a direct consequence of his promotion, Colin gained a new office close to Battersea Bridge in central London. This, in turn, was close to a public house.

Attending a business meeting one day at the former, Colin and colleagues then adjourned to the latter to spend an enjoyable evening downing a few ales. Eventually, with their after-work session at an end, Colin made his way back to his car prior to driving home.

"I'd left my car parked on a nearby street, but when I returned to the place I'd left it, it had gone—and with a boot-full of drink in it, too! Well, I went straight to the nearby police station to report it missing, only for them to tell me that the car hadn't displayed a valid parking permit so it had been towed away to a compound across the river. I'd drunk three or four pints that evening so off I went, staggering over the bridge and, believe it or not, even though I was pretty drunk and the car was loaded up with booze, they still let me have it back."

At a Crossroads

By 1976 Colin, now 40, was established as a successful sales manager. He was a leading light in the local Round Table, having become area chairman, and was heavily involved in organising and taking part in events and activities in his adopted home village. He was also a committed family man. Married to Norma and with two young sons, on the home front, too, it was a happy and busy time but also one of progressive change.

Jump-starting this change had been the family's 1972 move to a new home. The Reads had not moved far, just a few hundred yards, so although the switch was later to have a major bearing on the lives of all four family members, in the short-term remaining in Podington meant that they kept their village ties and the friendships they'd made there. For Philip and Jonathan staying in the village meant that they got to see out their primary education at Podington's school, the little educational establishment run by Miss Congreve.

Once that was completed, the brothers moved on to Harrold Priory Middle School, Philip first, then younger brother Jonathan.

In the 1970s this village school, which had previously educated pupils from ages 11 to 14, fell into line with the local authority's three-tier system and adjusted the age range to nine to 13. However, when the time came for the Read brothers to move on they went their separate ways with Philip winning a scholarship to Bedford Modern and Jonathan completing his schooling in nearby Sharnbrook.

Different schools, then, for the Read youngsters, who were quite different people, too, their father summing up his sons' characters as follows: "They've got completely opposite personalities. Philip's quieter, more serious, while Jonathan's more extrovert and, as a boy, was more excitable."

Their interests mirrored their differences. Taking more after his mother, in time Philip developed a passion for plants, an interest that would later take him to Pershore College, where he gained an HND in horticulture. Jonathan, on the other hand, had a fascination for computing, his programming talent evident even as a schoolboy.

A Bolt from the Blue

Meanwhile, back in the hot summer of 1976, as Britain baked, basked and sweltered in record-breaking temperatures, the Read family headed off on a foreign holiday. Before the births of their sons, and again after Philip was born, weeks away had often been spent in Cornwall, at picturesque coastal places like Veryan, but in July 1976 Colin, Norma, Philip (then aged 14) and ten-year-old Jonathan jetted off to Sitges in Spain. Returning to the UK early on a Monday morning, a few hours later, Colin was still in bed when a call came through on the home phone.

"We'd had a really lovely holiday, but our plane back hadn't landed until about 3am, so all I was going to do that day was have a lie-in and then pick up my new company car from just up the road in Wollaston. At about half past eight that morning, though, when I was still fast asleep, the phone rang. I got out of bed to answer it, and there was this American voice on the line that I recognised as belonging to the manager of the company that had just taken over Capital Cities. And this man says, 'Hi, Colin. I'm ever so sorry to bother you but, and I have to be frank about this, we're making you redundant!'

"I couldn't believe what I'd just heard, so I replied 'What? You can't do that!'

"But he just said, 'I'm sorry, Colin, that's how it is. Oh, and don't pick the new car up, just let them know you don't need it now and then come in and collect your stuff.'

"'The hell I will!' I said.

"But this guy kept trying to get me to call into the office. 'I'm not coming in,' I told him.

"'You've got to come in!'

"And so it went on until I lost my rag and said, 'You've got to be joking. You don't employ me now, and I've got something much more important to do today!'

"So then he says, 'What's that?'

"I was so cross by that point, I blurted out, 'Find another job, you stupid fool!' and slammed the receiver down."

And then, with the call over, the stark reality of his new situation washing over him, Colin sat down on the stairs. "I just sat there almost in tears when Norma appeared and said, 'What's going on?'

"I just looked at her blankly and said, 'I've just been made redundant.'"

The reasons behind his job loss Colin already knew, although he'd not expected the recent takeover of his firm to lead to him losing his job.

"Boeing, the giant US airline, had just bought Capital Cities Computer Services because they wanted to 'connect into' Britain," he states. "Of course, I was still selling my systems and services, but there was another department, run by Brian Mustoe's brother-in-law, which was running the latest interactive computer system, linking up with other computers in other parts of the world.

"Boeing found out about this and saw that this section of the company would provide the ideal opportunity to connect into Britain as part of its plans to establish worldwide network processing." As a result, the new American owner of Capital Cities Computer Services laid off all its batch processing sales staff.

Unemployment... for Four Days!

Knocked off the high perch of his successful sales job, Colin's star would soon rise again thanks to his Round Table connections.

"As things turned out, being made redundant in 1976 was the best thing that ever happened to me. For one thing, it got me thinking about working for myself, while in the short-term I soon found an excellent new opportunity."

But before starting out on his next job, there was some unfinished business to attend to: collecting papers and other bits and pieces from his office at Capital Cities.

This could have been a simple, tail-between-the-legs visit. Colin, though, had no intention of slinking in and out unnoticed, "Almost immediately after I'd been made redundant, Norma got talking to a couple of our friends, one of which was Michael Orlebar, who told her that his wife, Barbara, had just bought a new sports car. One thing led to another, and before I knew it Norma had organised that Barbara would pick me up from Watford after I'd finished collecting my stuff from my old office in Clarendon Road as she wasn't able to. It was a cracking car, and Barbara was blonde and beautiful. Why not? I thought.

"So she came and picked me up and, as I left the building, all the staff were looking out of the windows as I got into this sports car. Slipping into the passenger seat, my friend's very attractive wife leant over and gave me a great big kiss—which was all part of the act, of course. Then, as we raced off up Clarendon Road, I turned around and stuck two fingers up at all the gawping faces staring out from Capital Cities' windows!"

That same week Colin was back in work. His new salary was less than a quarter of what he'd previously been earning, and his new company car, a Ford Cortina, wasn't a patch on the model he'd been due to take delivery of on the day he was made redundant. Curiously, these details meant next to nothing to Colin as he prepared to sink his teeth into his new job as a salesman.

"I'd been told about this job by a Round Table friend in Peterborough, a man named Phil Wainwright, who was the managing director for a company in the town called Eastern Computer Services."

Eastern Computer Services, like another group firm, Cambridge Computer Services, was owned by Geest, the corporate giant, and it ran its operation using IBM mainframe computers.

"Eastern Computer Services were operating a conventional bureau similar to the one I'd just been involved with and so, to cut a long story short, I was offered a job. I think I'd been earning something like £20,000 a year with Capital, but the basic salary at Eastern was only £4,800. The company apologised that they could only offer me a selling position and a much lower salary. I didn't mind because of the bonus scheme that was part of the job package, so at the job interview I said, 'I'll take the job because I think I'll meet the bonus targets you've outlined.'

"The interviewer just looked at me and said, 'Nobody else has.'

"To which my response was, 'Fine, but I will.' And I turned out to be right."

Eastern Promise Realised

No sooner had Colin joined Eastern Computer Services than he was generating his first leads and selling business systems left, right and centre. So successful was he, in fact, that one particular team back at base knew exactly what was coming its way when colleague Read entered their office.

"I used to regularly walk into the room where the development and programming staff worked," Colin remembers, recalling conversations with the team's manager that would go something like this:

Manager: Hello, and what do you want Colin?

Colin: Well, I've come to see how busy you are.

Manager: We've got too much to do. You're giving us too much work, you know.

Colin: Oh, good… because I've got some more for you!

As the orders rolled in so too did the bonus cheques and, within six months of joining, Colin was earning as much as he had at Capital Cities Computer Services.

Then, after less than 12 months on Eastern's payroll, came promotion. "They sacked the sales manager, my boss, and gave me his job and his office," explains Colin.

With bonus targets and then promotion secured, and in double-quick time, in one respect this success had been achieved despite, not because of, his employer's approach to sales.

"I'd say that Eastern didn't have a strategy when I joined them. They had people called account managers and they went out to find 'prospects'. They were all middle-aged people, a bit older than me, and none of them had the word 'salesman' in their job titles—even though that's what, really, they were supposed to be. So I got them all together and told them we were wasting too much time going around explaining what the company did instead of selling our services. My view was that if I said someone was a salesman that's it, they knew they had to sell something."

As if to prove his point, a damning example of the company's previously woolly approach to selling came to light. "I'd not long become sales manager when I found out that one of our guys, an account manager, had been talking to a company about various computer systems."

Visiting the firm in question, Colin met the main contact there.

"I talked to this man and soon found that in all the time he'd been dealing with Eastern Computer Services, he hadn't once been told the company was trying to sell him anything! Our man had been talking about this and that option without actually ever coming round to saying 'Would you like to buy this system?'"

Altering the job titles of his sales team, coupled with the insistent focus on selling, reaped its rewards. The changes were indicative of the clear thinking, direct approach Colin had earlier brought to his selling role, one that's perfectly illustrated by a story Colin tells of a conversation he had with Eastern's MD.

"I was in a meeting with him one day when he asked me why I didn't use my entertainment allowance. My answer was that it was my policy to sell to the decision makers, people who didn't have the time to spare to be entertained drinking alcohol or tucking into three-course lunches."

In his managerial role it was this same single-mindedness that enabled Colin, by then in his early forties, to bring in more and more business. As sales manager, he also led by example when it came to commitment. In his own words: "I didn't go home on time, I went home when the job was finished." And so the company's turnover rose by almost 300 per cent in Colin's time in charge of the sales force.

Two Hats, Many Christmas Trees

Not content with driving up sales for Eastern, as the end of the 1970s dawned Colin continued to moonlight by devoting many hours to supporting Norma's Podington Nurseries project which, being a keen gardener, she had started up in 1976 in their garden. As he puts it, "My job was sales director of a computer company. My hobby, which took up as much of my time, was helping my wife develop her nursery business." Little did he know then where this would lead in a few years.

Easy to imagine, then, how this double life he was leading could, at times, be difficult. And, as one particular episode shows, splitting his time between two very different roles caused some unease and led to much self-questioning.

"In the early days of Podington Nurseries, we wanted to sell Christmas trees, and clearly, to make a profit, we had to buy and sell these in volume. And to get the volume, we had to seek out places that grew large numbers of good quality trees because it was important to us that our customers bought the best.

"I managed to find one place out Wisbech way, and I rang them up and agreed to buy 2,000 trees from them. To transport these we needed quite a big lorry, so I got a friend with an HGV licence to help me collect them. And in buying this vast quantity of trees, I did what I went on to do at the garden centre: I went a step further than anybody else would do. I ordered the trees without knowing where I was going to sell them.

"I didn't know where I was going to sell these trees, but I knew that I would sell them."

Having taken on this large consignment of fir trees with Christmas just a few weeks away there was no time to lose, and Colin wasted none in looking for buyers for his seasonal stock. Two petrol stations, including one in Corby, were soon persuaded to take 500 each. With half the stock accounted for, the next port of call was a Sunday market near Kimbolton. However, selling his Christmas trees there did not go to plan.

"I went there early, about five o'clock in the morning, to get set up, and I'd only just started to unload when the market manager turned up and said, 'You can't bring the rest into this part of the market, mate. Stallholders pay a lot of money for a place here. You'll have to go down there'. The area he wanted me to move to was right by the entrance."

Colin wasn't impressed by this last-minute change of venue, but the manager clearly wasn't for turning. The result? Colin moved his trees to the market's entrance area and got ready to launch plan B: attempting to sell his trees to the people walking past him on their way to the main market stalls beyond.

"I got my trees and I lined them all up and then talked to people as they came through the entrance," he recalls.

Despite the poor pitch, sales were pretty good, but even so the Sunday market experience evoked contrasting emotions. "I sold most of the trees and felt very pleased about that, but the whole time I kept trying to eye up the customers I was selling to, hoping they weren't going to be the same people I sold to at Eastern. The two roles just didn't go together at all. There was also this realisation that here I was, dressed like a farmer, on a Sunday morning at the beginning of December, trying to sell things almost literally off the back of a lorry to people who weren't really my customers."

A Lady in Distress

Colin's day job, however, found him with an increasingly pivotal role to play in the fortunes of Eastern Computer Services, and because of this he attended regular group meetings of the parent company, Geest, to deliver reports to senior management. Predictably, as the bringer of good news, the sales manager was a welcome speaker. Not that every meeting went so well…

"My report was always one of the highlights because they knew the figures I'd reveal meant they were going to get rich! And I was so pleased with myself that I used to hold the profit details back right to the very end. Generally, these meetings went off pretty well, except one time when things didn't work out so well. On that occasion, I'd set off from Podington to Peterborough, taking this short cut I knew. I was haring along in good time for the nine o'clock meeting until, that is, I was about ten miles from Peterborough.

"I was going down this narrow road towards Great Gidding when suddenly I came upon these two women standing by a broken-down car and rubbing their heads. It was almost a single-track road, and I couldn't have got past their car even if I'd wanted to so I stopped and offered to help."

It turned out that the car had a flat tyre, which Colin set about replacing. While he was doing so he talked to the car's driver and her companion and learned that they were heading to Peterborough to catch a train there. He also found out that one of the pair was not just a lady, but a Lady, although he can't now recall her full title.

Unfortunately for Colin, fitting the replacement wheel made him 15 minutes late for his morning meeting, so he made his entrance with the board meeting already in full flow. His day didn't get any better, either, as a director later reprimanded him. "This fellow came up to me and said, 'You're doing a good job, you know, but you shouldn't be late like that.'

"I said, 'I work more hours than nearly everybody else here.'

"His response to that was, 'Unfortunately, these people don't see that, though, do they? They only see that you've come in late to a very important meeting.'"

Super Secretary Enjoys a 'Royal' Wedding

As it happens, this story is one of two from this period with an aristocratic flavour. The second one begins way back, on the night Colin joined the Rushden Round Table, and picks up some time later, when he becomes manager of the Northants Computer Bureau, a new offshoot of Eastern.

"I'd taken over this bureau and it was a mess, and one of the main things I decided I needed was a good secretary. I soon found the right girl, Amanda, who was the daughter of Peter Neville, a good friend of mine and a man I'd known since 1962, when I'd gone to his hotel for the Rushden Round Table New Year's Eve party.

"Amanda was about 19 then, and this was her first proper job. She was working for me as part of a small team, and she picked things up pretty quickly. Then, when she left us, she got a job in Prince Charles's press office, eventually going on to become his press officer."

Some years later, Colin and Norma were invited to attend Amanda's wedding celebration, a high-society occasion that began in the chapel in the grounds of St James's Palace in London and ended at a grand function in a fine house down Richmond way. This venue had strong connections to Sir Winston Churchill, a man who coincidentally shares a birthday with Colin, whose memories of the glitzy wedding affair that day are typically laced with humour.

"A group of us had travelled up to London in a smart coach, the men all dressed in top hats and tails. We were some of the few non-titled guests, but we were dressed probably as smartly as they were, if not better. Anyway, once the celebration at the chapel was over, we went off to the reception. Before we left, though, we had to see off Amanda and her new husband."

This traditional post-wedding ritual had been given a royal twist as the Queen had kindly loaned the couple a stately, maroon-tinted limousine complete with miniature bonnet-mounted flags flying Her Majesty's colours plus a chauffeur to drive them to the reception venue.

"The car was absolutely immaculate," Colin recalls, "and the newly-weds were clapped and cheered on their way by all of us who were standing there."

With the couple then safely en route to their reception, the guests boarded their coach and followed on. However, it wasn't too long before the best-laid wedding plans began to go slightly awry. Travelling in their luxury coach, most of the passengers were busy talking with everyone, excited by the lovely day they were all having, while the coach driver made good time, taking advantage of every available bus lane. It was while the coach was proceeding along one of these lanes that Colin saw something unexpected.

"I happened to be looking out of the window when I saw the Queen's car that was taking Amanda and her husband to the reception. It was stuck in traffic, so I piped up and said, 'I think we're about to pass the wedding car!'

"There was a bit of laughter and then someone remarked, 'Well, we won't be received by the bride and groom now because we're going to arrive before them!' which prompted more laughter."

Sure enough, the guests did arrive first and were quickly ushered out of sight until the wedding car arrived. Secreted at the back of the reception building, the guests waited there hidden until, at last, the chauffeur steered the royal limo into the grounds and the guests duly emerged at the front of the venue to greet the late-coming newly-weds.

Another, very different, tale also dates from Colin's time with Eastern Computer Services and begins with a meeting between Colin and a services manager for Overseas Containers Limited (OCL).

"I was in the office of this very mild, calm little man selling some computer systems to him when we got round to talking about what we did in our spare time. And we soon found out that we had a common interest in sailing."

All at Sea

A short time later, the two men had agreed that Colin would join the man from OCL at Cowes, where his yacht was moored, with Colin signed up to be one of the crew as they raced the vessel in a regatta event. One Friday, as Colin took a train down to the south coast, he was looking forward to an enjoyable weekend of sailing and socialising. What transpired, though, was quite different, with warning signs evident soon after his arrival.

"I got down there all dressed for the occasion and carrying my holdall and a nice jacket and spare pair of smart trousers for when we went to the pub. As I was walking down towards the harbour, the evening sun was shining and I was in a good mood. One of the first boats I saw there was Edward Heath's yacht Morning Cloud. Then I came across this dishevelled-looking boat, which turned out to be the boat the OCL guy owned. I walked up to it, and this fellow said, 'You must be Colin.' I told him I was. He then said, 'Good,' grabs his bag and promptly jumps off the boat."

Twenty minutes later, along with three other men, the man from OCL pitched up, and within minutes of his arrival Colin was beginning to have second thoughts about agreeing to become one of this crew.

"He was very officious, nothing like the man I'd met earlier, and right away he made us all feel very uncomfortable. The others were going, 'Did you know what he was like?' and I told them that I'd not seen this side of his character at all."

The boat's crew got a further, early evening taster of their captain's approach when, at about half past six, the captain looked at his watch and made an announcement: "We've got to be up and away by 6.30 tomorrow morning, so we ought to have a snack now before we go to sleep," he said.

"Don't we get to go down the pub first, then?" Colin asked jovially.

The other crew members, caught unawares by Colin's insubordination, looked at each other and whispered but to their surprise the boat owner backed down.

"Well, it is Friday night, so I suppose a drink would be okay," he replied.

Yet even this more relaxed attitude was not quite what it seemed, as Colin recalls:

"We headed off to the pub with the 'captain' leading the way. When we got there it was full of people, full of blokes out enjoying their Friday evening, so this fellow starts literally pulling them to one side in order to get to the bar as we followed on behind.

"After he'd barged his way to the bar, he bangs a fist down on the counter and shouts out, 'Five halves of bitter, please.' Then, when I'd got my half, I'd only had a few sips when he suddenly says, 'Drink up.' And that was it. That was our evening in the pub!"

Things were no better the following day as boat and crew took part in their 34-foot class race.

Even as the men prepared the boat ready for sailing, the weather was appalling with strong winds raging across Cowes harbour.

Half an hour out from shore, their earlier fears were realised as Colin and the others fought to keep control in the teeth of a gale which, according to Colin, "was definitely blowing nearer force nine than force eight".

As the morning wore on, the effects of this constant struggle were all too evident.

"By midday I'd been hanging on to this rope for hours and my hands were bleeding. And still it was blowing like hell and we lost spinnaker after spinnaker, three of these large, loose sails in total. It was so stupid, this little man was throwing sails away like there was no tomorrow."

As the day wore on, hunger too became an issue so at one point Colin called out to a fellow crew member.

"There I am lying flat out on the deck, hanging on for dear life when one of the others came near. I shouted out to him, 'Have you got anything to eat?' He nodded and passed me a biscuit. A tiny, very thin biscuit that tasted awful. And that was it. That was my food for the day."

Happily, Colin made it back to shore in one piece. Finally released from this ordeal, he hurried off back to Podington just as fast as the trains would take him. Once home he took to his bed and slept for 12 hours straight.

The End of the Eastern Road

Five years after joining Eastern Computer Services, Colin quit. It had been a highly successful period for him, one that had culminated in him being appointed manager of the Northants Computer Bureau. That latter role proved to be a difficult one for him and, in 1981, he decided it was time to take the plunge into self-employment, a move he'd vowed he would make even before he'd joined Eastern.

"A number of us moved to Northampton, and we all found the style of the operation of the bureau there totally different to what we'd been used to in Peterborough. It wasn't being run how I wanted it to, people in the new company were suspicious of me, and I wasn't getting as much support from above as I might have."

As the new manager of an established set-up, Colin understood this response, but ultimately it was neither staff attitudes, working practices, nor even feelings of isolation that made him decide to leave. He'd been successful with both the Eastern and Northants businesses, but as in his last months with Marriott, he sensed change was in the air.

Again, too, the feeling that 'Good enough isn't' came into play, as Colin explains:

"I looked around, looked over my shoulder, so to speak, and there was nobody else as old as I was selling computers. And so I knew that my time was coming to an end so far as computers were concerned. Remember, I didn't even touch a computer button in those days; I just used to tell programming people what to do with computers and they'd do the rest. So I told myself that either I'd have to go back to the beginning, start out all over again, or I'd have to get out eventually. I didn't want to start again, so that was one of my reasons for deciding to quit. The main reason I left that job, though, was to work for myself."

One man was absolutely convinced he was making a big mistake. "I told my boss there that I was going to leave to work on our nursery business, and he just laughed and said, 'I know you've got your figures wrong. There's something funny going on because it doesn't make any sense that you're going to work for less than you've been earning here!'

"Then I told him something else. 'Well, it's like this, I'm also going to help run another family company called Podington Computer Services, and I'm going to sell small personal computers. You're still stuck with these great big mainframe things, but I'm going to sell the little ones."

Colin wasn't finished with computers quite yet.

A Tale of Two Businesses

To use a gardening metaphor, Podington Garden Centre was the eventual offshoot of what had begun in 1976 as Podington Nurseries, which itself had begun life as a

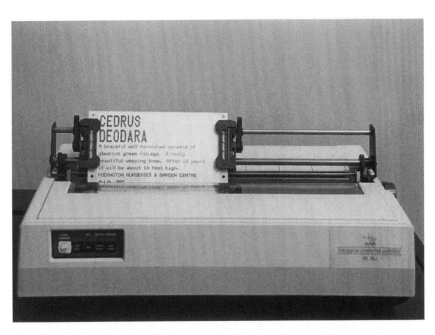

Label printer, used to great effect by the garden centre

small-scale, back-garden enterprise selling home-grown produce. The advent of the business had been a natural and planned progression following the family's move the short distance to 31 High Street. It was the site of Podington's former Co-op shop. The property, having been empty for quite some time, was in a sad state of disrepair by 1972, when Colin and Norma Read bought it for their new home.

"I'd taken on more than anybody else was prepared to do because I knew this contractor in Rushden who told me he'd produced no fewer than 24 estimates for people interested in buying the property," Colin admits before going on to declare, "Everybody I spoke to saw this place as a derelict building, which is what it was. I saw it as four acres of prime land."

With the family still living in their existing Podington home, thereby preventing its sale, work on renovating 31 High Street could not begin soon enough as, despite a fair income, the Reads' finances could not have stretched to owning two homes. Progress on the new property, however, could easily have come to a grinding halt.

"We'd got these plans to create a nice house with a big garden in which to grow stuff and sell it 'on the side', but we got hit by the fact that we couldn't claim back VAT, which the Government introduced in April 1973 at ten per cent. If I'd been a commercial builder in those days, I could have got the VAT back on the cost of the materials I had to buy to do up the house. I'd thought I'd be able to get it back, too, but I was wrong. It was the trickiest time I've ever had financially, and it cost me something like £7–8,000, which I had to borrow as a bridging loan from our bank."

While this was a setback, it also provided the Reads with a crystal-clear focus on what they wanted their future to hold.

"We decided to start a nursery to try to recoup the money we'd lost. Norma and I had always been interested in gardening and were keen on growing things, lettuce and other vegetables—and we knew we were very good at it! Of course, at that time, I was with Eastern Computer Services and I was doing all right, so I hedged my bets and stayed with them while we got our business started. I was putting in long hours selling computer services and then, in the evenings and at weekends, I'd work on developing Podington Nurseries, planting trees, doing the heavy chores and, later, trying to find places to sell our produce."

This was what eventually transpired. To get to that juncture, though, much blood, sweat and a few tears had to be shed, and all the family worked hard towards the one end. Financing the complete renovation of their new property was not the only obstacle the Reads had faced in the first years at 31 High Street, Podington. The state of the building also provided sizeable problems.

"I didn't know when to stop pulling bits down, but then, frankly, it was all falling to bits anyway. There were walls outside, too, that had fallen down, and there were areas of our land that were covered up with piles of rubbish because villagers had come and emptied their waste bags there! Nothing worked inside the house either. There were no utilities, no running water etc. It was worse than derelict."

However, thanks to a man called Farrow, not all was chaos and concern.

"Victor Farrow was a Bedford architect, and he was renowned for doing up churches and other old buildings so, as our place was a listed building, I got him to draw up redevelopment plans, and I used his experience and his drawings etc when I decided to knock things down, inject the damp-proof course or whatever."

Working to this plan informed and brought method to the renovation work on the old shop and bakery. Even so, after more than a year of renovation work, the Reads' next home remained a work in progress. Despite this, the family took the plunge.

"We actually jumped in when I saw the money running out. I managed to buy all the internal doors for £8 in a builders' sale and then, when we were in, we got the rest of the place into a liveable state just as soon as we could."

There was much to do and so, for a time, the house that was not yet a home had some unusual features.

"The staircase wasn't finished before we moved in, and, although the beds we all slept in were in the bedrooms, both the boys and the two of us had to climb up a builder's ladder to reach them!"

Henry Cooper Pays a Visit

One Sunday morning Colin was hard at work at the rear of his new home. When the property had been home to the village's Co-operative shop, the area at the back of the shop had, for years, been a working bakery, and it was here that Colin was busy mending the door of the old oven that had been left there when, suddenly, a familiar face appeared amid the soot, bricks and stone that were all that remained of the former bakehouse. The face belonged to Henry Cooper. Not the one-time British boxing champion, but a lifelong Podington resident.

"Henry appeared dressed in a greyish-coloured raincoat and a brown trilby with a feather in the trim, and he was carrying a shooting stick. A very distinctive little man, very articulate, he walked in, said, 'Hello, Mr Read,' and sat down on the seat of his shooting stick.

"He asked me what I was doing. So I told him, and he started to laugh. I said, 'Henry, what are you laughing at?' and that was when he told me his story, all about this oven of mine." The story Henry told Colin was of how he, like most other villagers in days gone by, used to pay a weekly visit to the old bakehouse that was now part of Colin and Norma's new home.

"All my life, right up until a few years ago now, I used to bake our Sunday loaf in there," Henry said, pointing to the oven. "The whole village did the same. We used to bring our Sunday loaf and put it in the oven, go to church, then come back, pick our freshly baked loaf up and take it home to eat."

But that was not quite the end of the story.

"He'd just finished telling me that tale when a twinkle came into his eye and he said, 'I always used to come out of church early, mind, and I'd run across the road to the bakehouse here, pick out the best loaf and head off before the others arrived!'"

This was no tall tale told by the short Mr Cooper either, for when Colin later came to help Helen Day, one of the elder stateswomen of Podington, write a history of the village, a similar account appeared there. However, in the history book version the mass Sunday bread baking was carried out as a gift to the villagers by the Co-op's baker.

An old baking oven was not the only antiquity found by the Reads in the first weeks and months after they took possession of 31 High Street as, on the land at the rear of the property, they came across a coin. It was not just any old coin of the realm either but a penny minted in 1772, by a curious coincidence the year in which the family's new home had been constructed.

From Rubbish Dump to Garden to Working Nursery

With the new house finally resembling a home, work was begun on the area at the rear of the property.

A tractor was bought and the land prepared by Colin and Norma, with a little help along the way from other family members including Colin's father and his father-in-law, both now retired from their railway jobs. And then, with work on the house and outside space more or less complete, the family had a home they could live in plus a spacious back garden. This garden served as a play space for Philip and Jonathan, although gradually the area was cultivated and planted out.

Many of the heavy-duty tasks fell to Colin, but the green fingers definitely belonged to wife Norma.

"We developed the land and started growing plants and vegetables as a family enterprise, and we'd sell them over the garden gate. It was just a cottage industry then," is how Colin describes the first small steps along a road that, years down the line, would lead to the establishing of a hugely successful family business.

By 1976, the nursery was ticking over well enough, even though the whole operation was still run from within the three-and-a-half acres that comprised the family's back garden.

"Everything then was contained in the garden. An outhouse housed chickens and sheep, and we had a shed with a little desk in, where we took the cash if someone bought something.

"There were beds laid out, too, and Norma would even walk around the perimeter of our garden and take clippings from the shoots of various plants that were straying over our fences from neighbours' gardens, pot them up and then sell the results!"

Sales steadily increased, thanks to a combination of repeat business ("we attracted people and they were satisfied and came back"), advertisements in the local paper ("an ad would say something like *Buy 10 Leylandii for a pound!*"), and a sign on the roadside gate featuring a little green gnome—a gnome who arrived in unusual circumstances and then never left.

"I was doing my sales director job when I met up one day with some marketing men from a London agency. I'd gone to talk to them on Eastern business, but at lunchtime we did what we usually did in those days after a meeting: we went to a pub for lunch. So there we were chatting away when one of the guys asked me what I did in my spare time. I told him about the nursery business and also happened to mention that we didn't have a logo."

Podington Garden Centre's first lorry, in 1987

A few weeks later, though, Podington Nurseries did have a logo, courtesy of the men from the agency. Following the chat they'd had with the big man (Colin) about the little nursery (Podington), they presented Colin with three sketches. One, featuring a garden gnome, appealed immediately to Colin and Norma, and so a logo was born, one that was transferred across when Podington Nurseries became Podington Garden Centre, and would endure right the way through to 2014, when the family business was sold.

Just as customer awareness grew, so too did the extent of the Reads' estate as patches and parcels of land to the rear of their property were bought up. These were not prime agricultural plots though.

"The land was absolute rubbish—terrible!" is how Colin remembers the often neglected, overgrown plots. There were trees that had fallen down through various diseases, including Dutch elm disease, and each person that had rented their own little piece of land, which we'd then bought, had let the hedges grow wild."

A Dip in Fortunes

As additional areas were bought up and tamed, so the Reads were able to grow more. They grew cut flowers, wallflowers, Christmas trees, bedding and vegetable plants, and the ripe vegetables they grew were picked and taken to sell at markets.

They kept chickens and sold the eggs and even owned budgerigars, just as Colin had kept canaries when he was a lad. As mentioned, sheep were bought, too, a small flock that would provide a memory that, to this day, makes Colin and Norma laugh out loud when they talk about it.

"We were due to be going out to a fancy dinner one evening, but that afternoon Norma and I decided we'd dip the sheep," Colin says. "So we got an old-fashioned iron bath, put it in the sheep's field and filled it with the dipping liquid. Then we rounded up the sheep, lifted each one up, dropped them in the dip one by one and wriggled them around so they were fully covered. It was already fairly late on when we got started, but there were only ten in the flock so we didn't expect the job to take too long. And we were right, until it came to dipping the biggest sheep. First off, we couldn't catch it. Then, when we did get hold of the blighter, it was bucking and bucking. Finally, the two of us managed to get it into the bath. "Norma was holding its rear end, and as we dropped it into the dip, I ended up going in the dip with it! I was covered in the stuff and Norma had also got it all over her. It said on the dip bottle not to get any of this stuff on your person, so we both looked at each other, said 'Knickers to the sheep!' and went back to the house to get the dip off us just as fast as we could."

The day was a warm one and, with nobody else around, they both stripped off and washed themselves down with water from a hosepipe. Concentrating on getting themselves clean, the two of them had lost track of the time, so what happened next completely took them by surprise.

"We were out on what's now the patio, frantically washing ourselves down with the water when, all of a sudden, our childminder turned up in the back garden—and there we were washing ourselves with water from a hosepipe with

134

Rear of number 31 with the sheep

absolutely nothing on! Well, I shall never forget the look on her face…"

Colin and Norma quickly covered up. And, having persuaded the childminder to stay, they showered (indoors this time) and dressed before hurrying off to their evening do in Huntingdon, the pair still giving off the less-than-fragrant aroma of sheep dip.

While the sheep dipping episode provided some light relief, the more so when looking back on it, down the next few years there were stiffer, more serious challenges to overcome. In the drought summer of 1976, for instance, an irrigation system that had been installed "went to pot".

The problem with the sheep then was not catching the beasts to dip them but keeping them alive. The Reads had not long since bought their first animals when, with green grass becoming ever scarcer, and even the leaves from nearby trees consumed by the hungry sheep, they had to buy in emergency feed to keep the new flock from starving.

Not One Company but Two

Despite the various setbacks along the way, Podington Nurseries had ticked along. It had established a solid, if small, customer base. Podington Computer Services, on the other hand, came flying out of the traps right from the moment of its formation in 1980. Initially, Colin was a roving salesman for this new business, while devoting as much time as he could to helping wife Norma with the nursery which, in 1981, was renamed Podington Garden Centre.

The horticultural business was not the only Read-run enterprise to involve more than one member of the family because, although Colin successfully sold the "little computers" he'd mentioned to his boss at Eastern just before he'd quit, it was Jonathan Read who played the leading role in Podington Computer Services. Just how key to its development Jonathan was is perfectly illustrated by an episode Colin delights in describing:

"The John Innes Horticultural Institution in Norwich, a very respectable outfit, decided it was interested in buying the computer and software package we were looking to sell, which, looking back, was amazing really. So I turned up on this particular sunny morning at John Innes, dressed in suit and tie with a computer in the boot of my car."

Looking forward to clinching Podington Computer Services' first major sale, he was shown in to meet his contact. But there was an immediate hitch, one that threatened to leave this potentially lucrative deal dead in the water.

"The business manager I was meeting understandably wanted to see the computer in action. So I set it up on his desk to give him a demonstration of all the wonderful things the computer and our software package could do. But could I make it work?

"Anyway, being the salesman I am, I had to think on my feet, and I said to the chap, 'I'm going to need to speak to our technical department and, if it's all right with you, it would be easier to do that if I could have a little privacy.'"

He was happy to go along with this, leaving Colin alone in the room. Then, just as soon as he'd shut the door behind him, Colin made his call.

"Well, our 'technical department' was my 16-year-old son Jonathan, who was at school in Sharnbrook that day. I phoned his school and asked the secretary if I could speak to him. Her reply was, 'Mr Read, you do know that Jonathan's doing a mock O level exam at the moment and can't come out of the exam room until he's finished?'

"My answer to that was that I had to speak to him urgently as it was 'a matter of life or death!'. A few minutes later Jonathan came to the phone, and I quickly asked him how to get the damned computer working. He was furious, couldn't believe I'd pulled him out of his exam. He just said, 'Switch it on and switch it off again for 20 seconds, then switch it back on.'

"Next thing I hear is the secretary's voice saying, 'Did you get what you wanted, Mr Read?'

"I said, 'Well, it's working.'"

There were two upshots to this episode. The first was that Colin ended up closing the deal with the John Innes Horticultural Institution. The second was a family stand-off. "Jonathan was so angry that I'd called him during an exam that he didn't speak to me for about a week afterwards," Colin says. When the teenager's anger eventually subsided, he returned to playing an important role in his family's two businesses. In fact, as his father explains, his youngest son, despite his tender years, effectively created and ran Podington Computer Services.

"It was his idea to create some software, which I decided I'd help to sell. At that time my wife was labelling plants with plastic labels and a felt-tip pen. Then one day Jonathan came up to his mum and said, 'You should produce some like this.' And that was when he showed Norma and me this program he'd designed."

This program resulted in the product that came to be known as Label It, which then became an integral component of the package that Podington Computer Services installed on the Commodore and Amstrad PCs it sold. Over the next couple of years, Jonathan, having by then left school, became the new enterprise's managing director, although he didn't call himself the MD. As the business grew, he travelled to potential buyers to sell his labelling software, and he also oversaw the work of a technical team comprising one full-time employee and one part-time worker. In Colin's words the three-way partnership worked well.

"As well as learning more and more about plants, Norma had started to specialise in the nomenclature of plants and had begun producing labels for the plants she was selling. This happened at the same time as I was about to start selling the Commodore computers. So the two ideas came together.

"Norma and Philip were brilliant at nomenclature, and Jonathan, who was about 15 then, embraced that in the software he created, coming up with Label It. The name speaks for itself: the product produced labels—and it was better than anything else on the market, especially where plants were concerned."

This development enabled users to produce clear, legible labels with information printed in fade-proof ink on a crisp, weatherproof material made by DuPont but sourced from the UK. This would later prove invaluable as Podington Garden Centre grew.

Label It was a highly successful enterprise—especially for DuPont—the icing on the cake came one day when, unannounced, a representative of the company turned up at the garden centre and told Colin that Podington was DuPont's best customer in the UK and presented him with a cheque in appreciation!

Two Becomes One

Eventually Jonathan turned all his IT know-how to devising and then developing the new garden centre's computer systems. Brother Philip's extensive plant knowledge, gained at Pershore College, enabled him to make his own distinctive contribution to the rise and rise of Podington Garden Centre.

Colin was devoting more and more time to the two family businesses, but soon came the realisation that the family should, as it were, put all its eggs in its horticultural basket. The computer side was wound down, and Colin gradually gave up many of his outside interests.

For years, he'd led a full life outside work and beyond the garden gate. There had, of course, been the long held Round Table involvement as well as his roles at Podington Cricket Club (both as secretary and Friday-night jazz man). There had also been two stints as a governor at his sons' old school, Christopher Reeves Lower School, because, as he admits, "I always seemed to get involved with everything." Colin also enjoyed a happy and fruitful spell as president of the Rotary Club of Rushden.

With many interests put to one side, however, all Colin's energy and expertise were now focused on making Podington Garden Centre a success. For this son of an engine driver, the tracks were clear, and now it was full

steam ahead for the Reads' sole family business venture—
Podington Garden Centre.

Colin at a Rotary group meeting

The Good Life Gets Better & Better!

When the Reads opted to change the name of the nursery business to Podington Garden Centre, the destinies of the four Read family members became inextricably linked.

Norma had continued to develop her knowledge of plants, while the different skills and characters of Philip and Jonathan made them, each in his own distinctive way, central to the family's working endeavours.

As for Colin, his time and business acumen were dedicated to ensuring that Podington Garden Centre became a going concern.

With the advantage of hindsight, it's easy to see a sense of inevitability about the Read quartet coming together to run the one family business. Their interests were similar and their skills worked well together.

Less obvious, perhaps, is the reason for the nursery's change of name and with it the formation of a limited company. It was not something that had been part of a fixed plan, rather it was a switch prompted by a conversation Colin had with a customer one morning.

"For some reason or other we'd decided to sell some seed packets, possibly Thomson seeds. Anyway, that morning a guy walked into the garden. We said hello to each other and chatted about this and that before he decided to buy some seeds. Then, just after he'd paid me, he suddenly said to me, 'You know you're trading illegally, don't you?'"

The customer then revealed his true colours, explaining that he was a local planning officer and that Podington Nurseries wasn't allowed to sell produce that was not home-grown. He then issued Colin with an ultimatum:

"You either become a garden centre or I shall have to close you down," he said.

"We'll become a garden centre then," replied Colin.

"It's not quite as easy as that," the planning officer continued, "you have to apply for permission first."

As things turned out, planning permission was granted, even though, as Colin emphasises, there were some objections.

"Our application caused quite a bit of unrest in the village. Some residents were very, very opposed to what we were proposing. One major concern was the fact that we intended to open on Sundays, but we still managed to get approval."

Lettuces + Loss = a Retail Future

If the decision to launch Podington Garden Centre was a big one, more momentous still was the decision to concentrate on retail.

Despite the family's lack of experience in the retail trade, Colin was sure retailing was the way to go, his mind all but made up by a near-disastrous early morning attempt at selling a van-load of lettuces.

"With more and more polytunnels, we found ourselves growing various different plants and we were particularly proud of our celery and lettuce. Of course, at this time, remember, I was still the sales director for a computer company in Peterborough, but one day I got up very early to head off to a daily fruit and veg market in Leicester."

Colin and Norma had found out that this was a place where professional growers went to sell their produce. So they'd decided to sell their now ripe crop of lettuce there, which meant the husband and wife team working different shifts in order to ensure the lettuces were picked (Norma's role) and delivered to the market (Colin's job). As the lettuces needed to be harvested in the dark to keep their lily white stems from turning brown, Norma worked through the night picking, bagging and boxing her crop. Once that task was complete, Colin loaded their delivery van and drove the stock to market. So far, so good. But there was a nasty shock in store.

"I'd put my old clothes on, loaded up our Bedford van and driven to market, all before five in the morning. But when I arrived at the place, there was nobody about. Then, after walking around the site for a while, I found the man who was in charge of this wholesale operation. I told him I had a van-load of lettuces to sell, but he just shook his head and said, 'Sorry, but you're too late. Everything's been sold by now.'

"I couldn't believe what he'd just told me, and so all I could say was 'But what about my lettuces?'"

"He just shook his head and said, 'I can't sell them. There's nothing I can do with them now.'"

A few moments later, though, the market boss changed his tune. Maybe he felt sorry for the man standing in front of him with a crop of unwanted lettuces, or maybe there was some other reason why he turned to the crestfallen Colin and said, "You know what, I'll give you 10p a lettuce."

This was hardly music to Colin's ears, yet the businessman in him also knew the sense in cutting his losses. Even so, it was a sombre, wiser man who made the journey back to Podington, where he put on his business suit, adopted his nine-to-five persona as a sales director and drove off to start another day's work with Eastern Computing Services. On his way, he was able to reflect on his market experience.

"Ten pence a lettuce didn't even cover the cost of Norma's harvesting effort, let alone yield any profit. At the price I eventually accepted, the load was worth about £4–500, but if I'd managed to sell it all properly at the market that day we'd have made £2–3,000. So I was more than a bit cross."

He was also more convinced than ever that the way forward was retail not wholesale, a conviction that had fully taken hold when, a short time later, he talked with a customer he knew near Northampton.

"When I met this guy I was still travelling all over the place selling strawberries or trying to sell lettuces or anything else we could sell. Well, this man thought he was the bee's knees, and he said to me, 'You shouldn't try and be doing business wholesale and retail. You want to make your mind up which you want to do.' So I told him that I'd been thinking a lot about what the business should look like and that we were coming out of wholesale and were going to take the plunge as a retail business."

Committing the newly fledged firm to this single market was a risk but, with Podington Garden Centre fully up and running, a period of dramatic and sustained growth soon followed, justifying this bold decision. It was a key phase in the business's development, one that Colin describes as "pivotal, a time when we started doing things properly". And there was an interesting postscript to this expansion:

"A funny thing happened after we'd been trading for about five years," Colin remembers. "I met the same planning officer who'd warned us about trading illegally, and almost the first thing he said to me was, 'If I'd known you were going to grow as quick as this we wouldn't have granted permission!'"

Good Enough Wasn't!

On their first day as a garden centre in mid 1981, the new company was trading from a small plot of land and an array of polytunnels. Customers back then would enter the site via the driveway at the side of the Reads' home, where a new sign had been put up informing visitors that they'd now arrived at Podington Nursery and Garden Centre. Inside, the products on sale ranged from fish and ponds to garden furniture and even a pool table. Despite its humble beginnings, the new garden centre bloomed.

Colin's belief that 'Good enough isn't' underpinned and fuelled the family firm's rapid expansion, but according to Colin there was another key ingredient. "At the time we started out, the tendency with garden centres was to specialise and to limit the stock in order to make more profit. To us that just meant there was an opening for somebody else to do the opposite. There are many, many examples I could give of how these big garden centres operated. One was the number of fruit trees they stocked. They'd maybe sell Bramley apple trees and Cox's Orange Pippin and a couple of others, and that would be it, with perhaps just two or three of each on sale." By contrast, the Podington way was to sell three different sizes of, say, 20 varieties.

"And we succeeded!" says Colin, "We didn't set out to be cheaper or more expensive than other centres, we just concentrated on being the only ones doing what we were doing, with Norma and Philip, especially, buying a wide variety of trees and plants. The diverse stock availability made Podington different from the other centres."

This remained the case throughout the many successful years the Reads ran Podington Garden Centre and, just as Colin emphasised in the video commemorating the 20th anniversary, the focus on "plants, plants, plants" was a priority throughout, from the small beginnings in 1976 right through to the sale of the business in late 2014. That stated, as Colin admits, there were many changes down the years.

"We bought up more land, put up new buildings, created a car park and introduced many new products, but plants were always the most important product.

"Others did things differently. They were run by retailers first and plants people second, and a lot of them found plants too difficult to look after. They only sold the plants they were selling a lot of."

This strategy was based partly on a philosophy that Colin sums up as follows:

"It was a well known fact that only 20 per cent of plants have common names and 80 per cent of the population only know these common names, so if you just try to sell the well known plants, you've got to do something magical to make a real profit.

"Well, we found a way to succeed by growing many of the plants people didn't know about, and we'd grow bigger, taller ones to show off alongside the smaller, shorter versions.

"Then, when a customer said 'Ooh, look at that camellia!' we could turn round and say 'No, madam, it's not a camellia, it's a so-and-so'—and that's how we'd get people interested in our range of new and unusual plants and trees.

"Take flowering cherry trees as an example. There are dozens of different flowering cherries, and so we stocked some of the less well known ones and they sold really well."

This approach required an extensive and informed knowledge of plants, which, of course, was something Norma and Philip Read had in abundance, but as the business developed, and more and more employees were recruited to Podington Garden Centre, the new front line staff also needed to know all about the unusual produce the centre was selling.

Buoyed by the strong sales, any profits were ploughed back into the business, with major expansion projects funded by bank loans. There was one important early purchase, however, that cost little but proved a real boon.

"After the initial planning application had been granted," Colin states, "we soon put our second one in for a permanent structure on our land. The application went through, and so I bought an old greenhouse, which was a low-roofed construction I'd found in a local farmer's field."

This greenhouse, which measured 100 feet by ten feet six inches, cost just £100. It was pretty rickety and needed a new roof, but once Colin had fitted that it proved to be a value-for-money buy, providing some much-needed undercover space to keep seeds and other products dry. The former greenhouse was also a place for keeping garden furniture.

Another key early investment was in flesh and blood, namely an accountant called Tim. Colin took pride in his accounting abilities, but from the outset he was convinced that the embryonic business needed a dedicated accountant.

"Finance-wise I was as qualified as anybody, but to the surprise of the rest of the family, the first person I employed was an accountant and I paid him more than I paid myself!

"The reason behind this was simple: my time was better spent developing the business and whatever else I needed to, so I let somebody else sit in the office doing all the adding up."

As for the four family members, they each had their own distinctly separate and salaried roles, all coming together for management meetings which typically, in the early days at least, were conducted while sitting down to an evening meal. In the meantime, other staff joined the business as it grew or when demand necessitated. Colin looks back on the centre's growth and sees how things evolved. As he puts it, "There was no one switch. It was, all the time, a continuing switch." Part of this was down to the fact that, unusually for the industry, staff were not employed seasonally but on limited-time contracts.

"We had a group of people working different hours and others working part-time. The key thing for me was that whoever was working, whenever they were working, they were part of a team. We always favoured this team approach so that knowledge was not limited to any one employee. Similarly, it wasn't important to me to keep the wage bill down just to make a few extra pounds because I didn't want us to make the biggest profit, but one policy I did stick to each and every year was to make more money than the year before."

The potential for increasing revenue might be seen as linked to a need to increase the size of the centre or to create or improve facilities. But, as Colin admits, there was one improvement that took considerable time to bring about.

"The location was always a stumbling block. You couldn't get lorries in very easily, so I eventually bought up some land which allowed us to create a new entrance and exit."

As mentioned, land acquisition was a common theme in the first decade of trading, with many of the 20 or more planning applications that were successfully lodged in this period being centred on extending the boundaries of Podington Garden Centre. What the company acquired was predominantly farmland, fields that were bought up in an expansion that Colin describes as "smoothly progressive", despite the fact that not everyone in Podington was pleased by the developments and some didn't like some of the changes that were a by-product of the garden centre's success. A particular bugbear was the volume of traffic and, in particular, issues with customers' cars blocking the village roads, so to help appease the neighbours the car park was significantly extended.

A VIP Comes a-Calling

There was one car, though, that villagers did welcome. This car was part of a small entourage of cars and motorcycles that passed through Podington one bright, sunny day. When the vehicle had set off a short while earlier, it's a nailed-on certainty that the driver at the wheel would not have expected to have been stopping in the little, out-of-the-way village that was Podington. But then the driver would have been unaware of Colin and his important contacts in high places.

"Ken Cooper was a very good friend of mine, a man who, like me, was in the Round Table. He was also the assistant chief constable of Northamptonshire, and he'd told me that, on this particular day, someone very special was going to be passing through our village."

That person was none other than Her Majesty the Queen, who was scheduled to visit a large farming estate that she owned in the Strixton area, just to the south of nearby Wellingborough. The royal party (Colin had learned from Assistant Chief Constable Cooper) would be in the area as it followed a route from the A6 via Wymington and on through Podington High Street, out on to the road towards Wollaston and the farm estate beyond. With this knowledge, Colin switched into action mode.

"There weren't that many customers at the garden centre that morning, so we decided to shut and asked all the customers who were in to go and stand at the site entrance by the road so they'd be able to see the Queen come through.

"In the meantime, I was about quarter-of-a-mile away waiting by the village church, keeping an eye out. Then along came some motorcycles, which parked at every junction, including the entrance to our garden centre."

A short time later, the Royal motorcade appeared and as the cars were spotted so excited voices cried out: "Here she comes! Here she comes!" At this point Colin remembers counting five cars with a passenger in the front one being his friend Ken Cooper. Then, as the small motorcade passed on through Podington towards the Reads' garden centre, Norma turned to her husband and asked him if he'd spotted the Queen, who was travelling in the back of the second car. Straightaway, Colin tore off up the road as fast as he could, chasing the royal party. Luckily for him, as he turned the corner a few yards from the entrance to Podington Garden Centre, he saw Her Majesty's car parked up right by the centre. Better still, as he reached the car he found he was just in time to take a photograph of the Queen as some local children handed her a bunch of flowers. From there the Queen went on to Strixton.

HM the Queen stopping at Podington on the way to Strixton

Good Enough Isn't

As long-time residents of Podington, the Reads were all too aware of the impact their increasingly popular retail business was beginning to have on the community, and they regularly reached out to their fellow villagers.

They could have offered discounts to the locals, but instead preferred to give back to the community by way of social events such as the annual Guy Fawkes' Night fireworks display.

Another, very different local initiative came about when Colin won the prestigious competition run by a national business federation with his catchphrase 'Good enough isn't' winning £20,000 to spend on a marketing project. Soon after the win, Colin began a major gardening project involving local schools. "My proposal to the competition organisers was that we'd give every school in the vicinity of the garden centre a seed tray, a bag of compost, some seeds and anything else they wanted to grow a garden in a tray."

Once these 'gardens' were in full bloom, all the school's entries were brought along to Podington Garden Centre to be displayed and judged. "The adjudication took place on a Saturday, and it was probably the busiest Saturday morning we ever had at the centre. The marketing for the event was really good, and so the place was packed, so packed in fact that we couldn't fully control the event. The car park soon filled up and then we had to let people park their cars outside.

"But it was great seeing the children turning up with smiles on their faces, and they'd prepared some beautiful work, too, which the small panel of judges I'd got together spent a long time assessing."

Colin

Colin at a Round Table President's Evening with
Wynford Vaughan-Thomas & John Coleman

In the Village of Podington.

Views of Podington in the early 1900s

This page & next: Number 31 High Street, Podington
in a state of rebuild in 1972.
Bottom right: Philip & Jonathan in their bedroom
in the middle of the rebuild

Aerial view of Podington Garden Centre &
Podington from the church, including number 31 High Street

Digby, the garden centre's mascot

Christmas display at Podington Garden Centre in the 1990s

Philip & Jonathan

This page and opposite: Aladdin in panto in the 1990s

Planting crocus bulbs for Rotary

Colin's sister Susan, who passed
away in 2011

The Read family

With Norma's retirement cake

Colin

Colin & Norma enjoying a cruise in January 2007

The Best Garden Centre presentation, 2014
& the certificate, opposite

North Thames Area Award

awarded to

Podington Garden Centre

For the

Best Garden Centre

Garden Centre Category

Standards Inspection 2014

presented by

The Garden Centre Association

GCA Chairman

Colin with a young garden centre employee,
showing that he knows his onions

The event also generated a lot of valuable press coverage for the centre, but, as Colin says, something more important came out of the project than mere publicity.

"It did wonders because young gardeners are difficult to 'grow'. You don't usually find people becoming gardeners until later on in life. They get more interested in planting then, but this project—and the prizes we put up for the winning schools and children—encouraged kids, which was the whole idea."

Of course, the school gardening initiative wasn't the only occasion the phrase 'Good enough isn't!' came to the fore. As revealed in this book's preface, these three little words were spoken by Colin in the 1996 video that Podington Garden Centre produced, but long before that 20th anniversary promo work the phrase had come to represent everything the centre strove to be, especially to Colin, as he explains:

"The phrase did not become a term in my vocabulary until I'd been at work a couple of decades or more. I'd always had the same attitude, the same feelings about how things should be done, I just hadn't expressed them in that way, and eventually I found there were more people saying 'That's good enough' than there were people saying 'I can do better'."

Applying this high ideal to his own endeavours was second nature and, as the garden centre developed and more staff were employed, so 'Good enough isn't' became a mantra for ensuring excellence. And for Colin, his belief in all staff providing exceptional service was perfectly demonstrated on a family holiday to Florida.

That's the Way to do it!

"We went to Disney World one year, and I saw there just how things should be done. The philosophy behind the place I totally agree with. For example, I'd just enjoyed a breakfast there that was about ten sandwiches high, and I was walking along looking for one of the attractions when I came across this boy sweeping away with a long-handled broom."

The tourist and the employee then engaged in the following exchange:

"Excuse me," said Colin.

"Yes, sir. How're you doing, sir?" replied the sweeper.

"Fine," Colin answered, "but I'm looking for the train ride."

"Yes, sir, that's a great ride," the boy enthused, "but it's real popular in the morning. Better to go on it in the afternoon, sir. The best time's about two," he added.

"So, after he'd given us directions, we went along at the time he'd recommended and there was no queue. And I've never forgotten that lad's face, or the brief conversation we had, which just summed up the whole feeling I've always had about how to run a business properly."

This principle of all employees providing the absolute best service possible could have proved difficult to embed among staff at the family's garden centre, especially where the part-time and occasional staff were concerned, but Colin believes the proof of the pudding was realised by the enduring success of the business, the loyalty of its employees and the awards and accolades the centre picked up down the years.

"I recognised that not everyone's the same and they have to be encouraged to do better or to do something differently. And yes, the staff got used to me saying 'Good enough isn't', and we supported them with training and so on, so we tried to help them be as good as they could be."

There was one Christmas, however, when this desire to bring out the best in staff came unstuck as Colin realised that the seasonal stock of Christmas items had been over ordered, so much so that Colin needed to have a word with the employee responsible, using the 'Good enough isn't' line of course.

The problem was that the double stock had already been put on show, therefore preventing other lines from being displayed.

After pointing out the problem, Colin wanted to leave it there, but the employee emphasised how sorry he was and aplogised again that he'd let the company—and Colin personally—down.

Colin accepted his apology but eventually the employee moved on of his own accord.

Tip-Top Customer Service

As time went on Podington Garden Centre focused more and more on informing and advising the many customers who visited. The information desk stocked scores of leaflets about plants, leaflets tailor-made for the business by the business. As Colin himself says:

"More and more customers realised that the information desk was the place to go, the place to find out

Podington Garden Centre displays in the 1990s

about our plants before they began walking around the centre. They'd come up and ask 'Have you got any heathers, winter-flowering heathers?' To start with, many people didn't really know the difference between one heather and the next, so one of the information desk team would take them in hand.

"'If you'd like to come along with me?' they'd say, and then they'd take them to where the heathers were, all the time asking the person questions."

This gentle but intelligent probing was intended to ensure that the customer not only bought plants but bought the right plants for them and their garden.

"As well as asking questions about the customer's garden and its soil and so on, the employee would also explain how a particular heather would grow better in his or her garden. The customer might accept that this heather would grow better, but then they'd point at another plant and say, 'I'd like one of those red ones'.

"Our member of staff would then say something like, 'Well, you've just said you live in such-and-such place down the road, and unfortunately the ground there's not really conducive to growing the red ones. So probably best you didn't buy that one.'

"We'd then explain that if the customer lived in Woburn, for example, that the place is full of them, so red heather would be a perfect plant to grow there."

As a consequence of this thoughtful and knowledgeable face to face approach, Colin believes that customers felt appreciated and informed, whether or not they spent any money at the end of their day's visit to the centre.

"Most people realised that we were not trying to put them off buying something, we were actually encouraging them to buy the plants that would thrive where they, the customers, lived and where the flowers and shrubs etc were going to be planted. And, of course, we also encouraged our staff to stress to customers the importance of keeping the plants' labels."

These labels, which had, of course, been early innovations jointly created by wife Norma and son Jonathan, had remained a central ingredient in Podington Garden Centre's winning recipe, each one featuring key information about how best to look after a particular plant.

Amusing Customers & Unwanted Visitors

Despite the outstanding and individualised support the staff offered, not every customer could be easily helped. One particular chap that Colin has fond memories of was a local man, a regular customer who became well known to the staff and to Norma Read.

"Norma and I always smile when we remember this fellow.

"A Cockney, he had moved from London to Rushden and hardly knew what a garden was. He kept coming back to buy seeds and plants, and one day he came in and went up to Norma in the information centre.

"'Hello, Mrs Read,' he said, 'I'm growing lettuce plants from those seeds I bought here and they're doing ever so well, so I just want to know when I should stake them.'

"My wife was puzzled by this, so she said to him, 'Sorry, what do you mean 'stake them'?'

A Podington Garden Centre leaflet

"And the fellow then explained, 'Well, they're up to here,' holding a hand about three feet off the ground. At this Norma couldn't help being amused because, as many, many gardeners know, she knew that if a lettuce plant's grown that tall it's well and truly gone to seed."

Norma and this customer became firm friends, and he returned again and again to be welcomed by the staff, who always recognised him when he dropped by.

Such loyal customers and other members of the public made up the lion's share of the garden centre's customer base, but businesses and organisations such as East Northamptonshire Council also bought Podington's plants, although having to abide by that council's rigid payment terms meant that, in real terms, profit margins were often lower than those made from selling to individuals paying by cash at the centre's tills.

Still, whether commercial or not, all customers were welcome. There were other visitors, though, who were very definitely not welcome.

"We used to sell a lot of fish, with the most expensive ones being the koi carp. And there came a time when we realised somebody was stealing our carp. Obviously we tried to catch whoever it was and eventually we succeeded. On that particular day, I was working as usual when one of the staff rang me and said they'd found out who it was and that the man was near the aquatics area with some fish stuffed in his pockets. I tore over and ran up to the bloke I'd been told about.

"Then I stood right in front of him and said, 'Excuse me, can you empty your pockets, please?'

"He just stared at me, said no and ran off with two large koi carp sticking out of the pockets of his coat. He must have been absolutely stupid to think our carp would survive being stashed in his pockets, but although he'd stolen some expensive fish—and we reckoned he'd been taking them for a while—at least he didn't come back to steal any more."

In addition to occasional daytime thefts, the Reads' garden centre had its share of after-dark incidents, with occasional nights disturbed by the sound of burglar alarms ringing out yards from the family's home. One night, Colin was woken by just such an alarm and went to investigate.

"It was after midnight when the alarm went off. So Norma and I pulled on some clothes and off we ran to see what was going on. It had happened before and we were usually the first on the scene. You'd get a bit worried when you got inside the main building as you'd be thinking whether you were in front of the intruder or behind them.

"Anyway, on this occasion, we made our way through the front door and almost immediately could hear this odd noise. Then we heard it again… and again. Just then two policemen arrived on the scene. One of them told us to stay back and, both a little apprehensive, they went to investigate. A bit braver by now, we followed them at a distance.

"Then, a few moments later, one of the policemen turned back towards me and said, 'It's all right, it's all sorted now.' And as he said that, we could see his mate holding the culprit: one of our white rabbits that had somehow got out of its cage and tripped the alarm!"

The follow-up was similarly amusing because when the constables came to write up a break-in report, it described how the pair had attended Podington Garden Centre where a robbery was believed to be in progress and managed to apprehend the suspect and banged him up.

The Workforce

In the 33 years the Read family ran their garden centre they were blessed with many loyal employees who stayed with the company for years and years.

Others stayed for just a short while, although typically even these short-term members of staff bought into the centre's quality service philosophy, with many work-experience lads and lasses, interns and other contract employees impressing Colin during their time with the company.

"Many of the school work-experience boys and girls were brilliant. They accepted the challenges we gave them and did ever so well.

"There was one guy in particular who turned out to be really, really good. He stayed on with us for a while after he'd left school.

"There was another lad, too. He was on a year's leave between jobs with the RAF.

"This lad wanted to be a pilot and had been shortlisted for a place in the Red Arrows team. He was another one who was brilliant.

"Unfortunately, I couldn't stop him going back. Not that I ever said to him 'Stay here and don't be a pilot!'. I tried to help him as much as possible while he worked with us, and we had some interesting conversations before he left. Plus he was kind enough to say that he'd enjoyed being with us and it had been a good experience for him. He was a great person to have around.

"He never did become a pilot, though, but stayed on in the RAF as an admin officer."

Another staff member Colin remembers with affection is a man named Nicholas Warliker. When the two men first met, Nicholas had just been made redundant from his first job. He'd been employed at Barnwell Manor, the Northamptonshire estate of Princess Alice, Duchess of Gloucester, which spanned approximately 11,000 acres. Nicholas had worked for Princess Alice for 25 years and was head gardener at the time the family had to leave the manor for financial reasons.

"He'd been earning very little money there and had only worked for the princess, so when we met I caught Nicholas slightly on the hop by offering him a job. He was thrilled to bits and turned out to be a fount of gardening knowledge.

"Mind you," Colin adds, "he could talk all day with one customer about just one plant! But he was great, Nicholas, and he became a trusted member of the team."

Nicholas kept in touch with Princess Alice. When he visited London, he was always welcomed at Kensington Palace, where the princess resided after leaving Barnwell. He would enjoy a cup of tea with the princess and was allowed to park his car at the palace while he visited the flower show. The princess passed away in 2004, at the age of 102. Nicholas was invited to the funeral.

Whatever the staff member's background, and however long they stayed, as the business grew so too did the overall number of employees, both long-stay and short-stay staff. At its peak, Podington Garden Centre had 70-plus people on the payroll in addition to the four family members. This disparate workforce, made up of full-time, part-time and contract workers, together with the interns and work-experience youngsters, all had to be properly managed and trained, a fact Colin clearly recognised,

"As we expanded and became more successful we took on more staff, local people within a 15 to 20 mile radius of the centre, but who typically lived within seven miles or so of Podington. Of course, we had to become more structured in how we looked after our employees. We had some very good ones who stayed a long time with us, and we had some very good people who trained our employees and made sure they had the skills they needed."

Valley, Peak, Valley, Peak

For Colin the drive to excel and improve was innate, but a speech he listened to in Manchester one day reminded him that even the most determined, most talented individuals can find it tough to continually repeat previous successes.

"I was at the Garden Centre Association (GCA) annual conference, and the main speaker, who was a coach of some of the leading British athletes at the time, talked to us about highs and lows in performances.

"As he said, he'd take his athletes to the top of the mountain to win a race or a field event, but then he had a problem: how could he motivate them to win next time they performed?

For him it was always 'mountains and valleys'. If a member of his elite squad won, he realised that they'd got to the top of a mountain, but then they had to go down the mountain and into the valley below. And no end of people, when they go down the mountain on their way to the next peak, lose their way in a valley and don't ever get back up again. So, as the coach pointed out, for him the most difficult time was often when an athlete was performing to a very high standard."

This resonated with the Reads' work at Podington Garden Centre and the challenges presented there in managing and motivating the staff. Yes, the best turnover yet may just have been achieved. Yes, PGC may have been awarded the independent garden centre of the year title three times. However, Colin always stressed that these achievements were not enough—he always wanted more, wanted the centre to be better the next year and better still the year after that.

Independent Status, Independent Nature

Progress wasn't just dependent on improving standards of service or employees' performance and productivity. Ploughing their own furrow, to use a horticultural term, came naturally to Colin and company, but this independent streak was matched by a willingness to embrace innovative new ventures. The centre's commitment to 'plants, plants, plants' never wavered, but when the time was right to change tack, change was made. In any case, the focus on plants was not an all-consuming, blinkered one. While the outdoor displays showcased a wide range of shrubs, ornamental trees, alpines, heathers, winter and summer bedding plants and aquatic plants, elsewhere within the centre, as mentioned, unusual cold-water fish and various pumps and other pond equipment were on sale together with a large selection of fountains, statues, fencing, tools, specialist garden equipment, composts and more.

The changes in direction that were made were inspired by a whole range of factors, with fact-finding foreign trips providing their fair share of food for thought and bright ideas.

One successful innovation was introduced following one of Colin and Norma's first working holidays, their 1993 visit to Australia. This trip was organised by another successful family-run firm, Colegrave Seeds, a British company still trading, although today known as Ball Colegrave. Going Down Under, the Reads were struck by an idea that was proving highly successful one day a week at one particular garden centre.

There, every Wednesday was Ladies' Day, the centre offering incentives to all women customers who shopped at the centre on that midweek day. Copied at Podington on the Reads' return to the UK, this simple, yet highly effective concept—including, for example, offering women shoppers a free cup of coffee for a minimum of £5 spent on produce—drew in many new female customers, thereby giving a much-needed boost to midweek revenues. Colin recalls that, on several occasions, one male customer, well known to Colin, told him that he was discriminating against the male race. Colin replied "Please sue us!" hoping for some good publicity. Of course it never happened.

There was another benefit, too, as Colin explains:

"I have this theory that if you go on a holiday, or a working trip, and come back with one good idea, just one, that's a success. And the best idea we got for the business on our travels was Ladies' Day. Our weekends at that time were so busy, especially on Sundays, that on some days you couldn't get into or out of the village. But within a year of starting our Wednesday women's days, our turnover had really increased and we'd solved the problem with weekend traffic in the village… Our village location had actually been putting people off from coming to visit us on Saturdays and Sundays, but Ladies' Day helped remove that barrier."

Tackling the predictable drop in weekday income by offering incentives to female shoppers was an initiative that worked, and in the early years there was another, even more significant, if predictable, dip in cash flow. Again, though, a new idea yielded up a moneymaking solution.

"Early on we were losing money from around October through to March. To a large extent we'd make up for this fall in income in the spring, but each December things would still get very uncomfortable. Our answer to this dip was to do something radically different and, for the first time, to branch out into an area that was only partially horticultural."

The centre's new creation was a Christmas event. The decision to turn the garden centre into a winter wonderland that December proved a hugely successful one, and from that moment on the annual Yuletide attraction—complete with Santa's grotto and, one year, live reindeer—was established as a fixture each festive season.

Down the years, countless other events were put on, the money and publicity raised by these contributing to the year-on-year expansion of the business.

Entrance to Podington Garden Centre

Changing with the Times

If a company is to survive and thrive not just for a few years but for more than three decades, then it has to adapt. Ladies' Days and themed Christmas events reaped rewards for Podington Garden Centre, while the decision to sell garden machinery did not.

Win or lose, the Reads' enterprise also had to continue to roll with a number of market changes, some of which struck right at the heart of their business.

"The biggest change in the period we ran Podington Garden Centre, and before that the nursery, was the decreasing size of gardens," Colin asserts.

"All the new houses that were being built had smaller and smaller gardens, gardens that'd have just a few plant pots in them.

"As time went on, I'd drive around the area and everywhere I went I saw new houses with one large pot with a plant in it by the front door and maybe three large pots around the back. And that was it."

Responding to a trend that could have had a fundamental effect on sales had the business chosen to ignore it, the response was not to diversify—for example by stocking more garden furniture—but to stand its corner, retaining its individual approach and emphasis on selling 'plants, plants, plants', and always providing the personal touch.

As Colin puts it, "We were saying, you buy the plants and we'll recommend what to put them in, where to put them and how to look after them. We might have made more money by selling other things, but we always concentrated on stocking and selling the widest range of plants."

Despite the external prompts to change, be they new ideas or different trends, there was, at the core of Podington Garden Centre's business strategy, a belief that up-to-the-minute and accurate management information was key to shaping decisions.

Colin was certainly convinced that, with so many variables to manage, no modern business could survive without a sophisticated management information system (MIS). The management and computer information department, headed up by Jonathan Read, produced both the pamphlets and books displayed in the information centre together with copious in-depth reports on customer-flow patterns, sales per visit/per square metre, plus analyses of stock losses, labour costs and detailed assessments concerning the effectiveness of advertising and promotional campaigns.

Spreading the Word

In the days before the World Wide Web revolutionised the way businesses promoted their wares and services to current and potential customers, firms like Podington Garden Centre relied on time-honoured, tried-and-tested ways of promotion, whether that be word-of-mouth recommendations or printed articles and advertising.

"We used the local press all the time. When we started out, newspapers were a lot more powerful than they are now. Even in the early years of Podington Nurseries, we placed simple ads to sell our products, so pretty much from the start of the garden centre business we wrote or featured in articles for the local papers. Then we had our own column, which saved us from spending some money as we didn't have to pay to promote what we were selling."

This regular media publicity not only kept Podington Garden Centre consistently in the mind of the area's green-fingered residents, it also sparked a phone conversation between Colin and a journalist that went like this:

Colin: Hello, it's me again!

Journalist: Hi, Colin, and what are you up to now?

Colin: We've just put a village pub in. (This was Norma's idea.)

Journalist: What d'you mean 'put a village pub in'?

Colin: Well, we call it a pub, a plant pub.

Journalist (curiosity piqued): A plant pub? What on earth's that?

Colin: It's a display that features these plants that attract insects, which drink the nectar from the plants—so much nectar, in fact, that they get drunk!

Local media connections and outlets were invaluable. Then, as the business grew, interest was drummed up further afield. A good example of just how far word eventually spread came when Podington Garden Centre gained great free nationwide publicity by hosting an episode of the BBC's popular and long-running radio show, *Gardeners' Question Time,* in which Philip Read was interviewed by presenter Peter Purves—a prestigious and highly valuable bit of publicity for Podington Garden Centre.

Bigger & Better—& Bigger Still

Ladies' Day, Christmas extravaganzas and a 'plant pub', these were all winning attractions, but none of these required additional space. As the mainstream business grew, however, space was often at a premium, and the centre's expansion continued.

"We must have put in more than 20 different planning applications as we developed the business, but of these, I think, probably five or six were really major, significant ones that were concerned with buying up extra land and building on it, or putting up or extending new buildings."

However, acquiring additional land did not always involve spending hard-earned cash as Colin's cordial relationship with Christopher Reeves, the leading local farm owner, led to some mutually beneficial land swaps. Swaps of land notwithstanding, there were still plenty of building projects, extensions and upgrades that did require heavy cash outlays.

"We were always looking to grow, and every year we seemed to put another extension in here, another development in there. In fact, as time went on, we even started making them two storeys high. It wasn't just about building more or expanding the square-footage of the site, though. Often it was about building better, improving what we already had."

As the site was developed, the customer experience was improved by installing or upgrading key facilities such as toilets, major car park extensions and the introduction of a café, which proved to be as popular as it was money-spinning. For Colin, creating or upgrading amenities like the café and toilets were essential steps forward.

"There's no doubt that places of interest, where visitors might spend several hours shopping or browsing, require somewhere for customers to eat and use a toilet. And the better the coffee shop, and the better the food and service, the better the business does. They tend to be related one to the other."

Not that the café the centre ended up running was the same as the one that had first been established. That had been a small affair, with the catering carried out by a local woman called Muriel who, according to Colin, turned up each morning with a bagful of food and drink. She'd then make and sell sandwiches, teas and coffees, in the early days serving just a handful of customers each hour.

Later, a larger version of the centre's café was given its own title, The Gnome's Kitchen, named after the gnome that featured in the garden centre's logo. This coffee shop sold home-made pastries and light meals.

Speculating to Accumulate

Podington Garden Centre was developed gradually, yet despite the growth being more evolution than revolution there were always times when tidy sums of money needed to be spent, enabling the centre to be developed and to generate additional income.

"We were always borrowing money to fund the expansion," Colin concedes. "We did it carefully, though, and, as a result, almost every new project would end up making more money than we'd originally borrowed to get it up and running. In any case, it was always acknowledged by everyone in the family that, if we did make a profit, we'd pay out dividends to the four family members and then spend the surplus and more the following year on developing the business."

As for the regular borrowings he refers to, these were always arranged with the business's bank, via the same branch that, years before, had stumped up the loan to buy the land for Colin and Norma's first home in Fenny Stratford. Some two decades later, that same bank manager, Mr Smith, paid a visit one day to the Reads' garden centre.

"I can remember him walking through one of our greenhouses, then after that we passed a concrete statue marked up at about £200. At this time I was looking for the bank to give me a loan of £2–3,000. Anyway, he tapped this statue and said to me, 'Do you sell them?'

"So I said, 'Well, yes.' Then he asked me how many we'd sold, and I couldn't lie so I told him the honest truth. 'Those particular ones we haven't sold many of.' Mr Smith stared straight at me then and asked me why we were stocking them then and at that price too? And I told him. 'Because we sell the full range and that one might lead people to buy other, slightly cheaper statues.'"

The bank manager, with a smile on his face, didn't seem impressed by this sales logic, but the bank still agreed to the loan.

Colin's Greatest Achievement

By the early 1990s there had been more than 20 failed attempts to repeal an act that for decades had placed stringent restrictions on Sunday trading in the UK. The act in question was the Shops Act of 1950. Then, in July 1994, pro-change campaigners—including Colin—were able to celebrate as Parliament passed the new Sunday Trading Act, which radically changed what could and could not be bought and sold on a Sunday in England and Wales; outlined entitlements for employees working on Sundays; and permitted larger stores to open for a maximum of six hours.

For Colin, his role in helping to persuade the country's lawmakers to make these changes, ranks as his finest achievement. But how did he come to be involved, and what exactly was his role? "When I'd worked for Robert Marriott, I'd sat on various government committees. Then, when companies like Sainsbury and Tesco wanted to lobby Parliament on getting Sunday trading laws changed, I was asked to join the campaign. This I did, and together with another garden centre's representative, I featured in a video. This 15-minute video was then shown in the House of Lords's common room.

"The two of us also went to the House personally. A 'pro-Sunday trading' lunch had been arranged, and we got to talk informally to the lords and ladies there about why we wanted the Sunday laws changed."

Colin was convinced that the pro-Sunday movement had the facts to back up its arguments, believing that businesses like Podington Garden Centre had the right to trade on Sundays, selling plants and other produce just as they did on the other six days of the week.

On the day of the big lobbying event, the architect in Colin didn't think much of Pugin's famous Palace of Westminster interior—it was "dull and windowless"— but he has fonder recollections of a memorable, if short, exchange he had, once inside the famous building, with a lady member from Scotland. He remembers the conversation as follows:

Lady member: Hello, Mr Read. Thank you very much, I had a very pleasant lunch.

Colin: Never mind the lunch, Madam. Do you think the new trading act will get passed?

Lady member: Oh, you'll have no bother at all with that. No trouble at all.

And the lady from north of the border was right as, on 5 July 1994 the Sunday Trading Act gained royal assent with the new laws taking effect the following month.

A South African Adventure

The year 1996 was a landmark one for Podington Garden Centre, marking as it did the 20th anniversary of trading since the creation of Podington Nurseries. In the intervening two decades the Read family had established its business as one of the UK's leading independent horticultural operations.

As touched on earlier, this achievement was commemorated by the release of a promotional video with commentary provided by Tom Baker, the actor best known for playing the role of The Doctor in the perennially-popular BBC series *Doctor Who*.

1996 also saw Colin and his wife jet off to South Africa. By then 60 and a vice-president of the International Garden Centre Association (IGCA), Colin flew there, accompanied by Norma, to attend the organisation's annual congress, the week-long trip taking in stays in Johannesburg and Cape Town.

For Colin and Norma this was the first of five foreign IGCA congresses they attended. Like subsequent get-togethers, this one featured formal meetings and talks interspersed with outings to local places of interest, including time spent out in the mountains and in the bush.

"We were one of three couples that went on a trip into the Drakensberg Mountains," Colin explains, "and when we reached our lodge, we found out it was miles from anywhere, miles and miles from anywhere. Then, one day we were driven off even farther out, to a plain where one of the great Boer War battles was fought. It was also a place where you could actually find gold. Tiny bits, but still gold."

As well as giving the couples an opportunity to see the country's interior, the excursion provided Colin with some close-up-and-personal encounters with some of the native wildlife for whom this part of South Africa is home. The first of these came early one evening when the party was taken out into the bush in their guide's Land Rover. They'd no sooner got there than Colin had to excuse himself.

"We were all sitting there at this spot where the guide had put a table and chairs out, eating snacks and drinking, when I realised I needed to 'go'—and in a hurry—so I asked the guide where the best place to use as a toilet was.

"I expected him to suggest somewhere close by, but he pointed into the distance and said, 'You'd better go over there,' adding, 'we won't look.' So I wandered off, found an out of the way place about quarter of a mile from the group and had a pee. Then, just as I'd finished I looked up and saw at least 150 pairs of eyes looking right at me. They weren't human eyes, though, but the eyes of a great herd of wildebeest!" Colin made a hurried exit from that scene.

This wasn't the first encounter with African animals he'd had on this journey into the South African wilderness. "Right at the beginning of our time in the bush, one party decide to go fishing with the guide. Norma and I didn't fancy that so we stayed behind at our lodge along with the caretakers.

"It was nice, but nothing special, and so the two of us decided to go off for a walk on our own that day. We were advised that where we were likely to be there were no dangerous animals, so at ten o'clock that morning off we went. It turned out to be a bit of a trek but it was ever so interesting.

"We came across a few snakes, but they'd buzz off when we came near. Other than that we walked and walked, taking in the views and looking at all the trees and plants.

In South Africa at Stellenbosch Vineyards

Then, all of a sudden we heard this noise, a grunting sound and quite loud. Neither of us knew what was making the noise, but I decided to copy it. And the sound came back at us. I said to Norma, 'I wonder what that is?' and then I made the noise again. When the noise boomed back at us a second time, we realised that the animals that were making it were all around us, even though we didn't know what they were.

"Then I caught sight of one of them: it was a baboon, one of a group of baboons that were hopping around in the bushes right next to us."

New Century, New Hobby

In 2000, at the age of 65, Colin did what many do at that stage of their lives: he retired. Or rather, he didn't.

He did cut down on the number of hours he devoted to work, although he still put in 30 to 40 hours per week as he retained his mustard-keen involvement in the family business.

With Norma by then fully retired, husband and wife found time to make frequent visits to their new timeshare property in Portugal's Algarve region, leaving the day-to-day running of Podington Garden Centre in the capable hands of Philip and Jonathan.

In the years immediately before his semi-retirement, Colin had taken up golf. A late starter, he quickly took to the game and became a member of Rushden Golf Club. However, it was in Portugal, at the grandly named Pine Cliffs Golf and Country Resort, that he really started to enjoy his new found hobby.

Enjoying golf at Pine Cliffs, Portugal

"Pine Cliffs is a beautiful place. We used to go in June each year. We had some lovely times there and, for some reason, I played golf better in Portugal than I did in England, although I never did get a hole in one in either country!"

Even so, Colin's golf "got better and better", and, in June 2009, this improvement saw him finish second on the Members' Golf Tournament Day. Two years later he went one better in a Pine Cliffs tournament. This win, the most memorable of Colin's years as a golfer, was also his last and was achieved on 21 June 2011 in that day's tournament. Carding the best score over two rounds of the nine-hole course spectacularly perched on the cliffs that far below were crashed into by the waves of the Atlantic Ocean, Colin was elated—and not just because he'd won the club's weekly tournament.

"Because I won I got to be invited back to Pine Cliffs the following February, along with the other 30-odd weekly tournament winners that season, for the resort's Golf Winners' Cup, plus there was a free week's holiday at Pine Cliffs."

Another part of the prize saw Colin automatically entered into the Champion of Golfing Champions tournament with the winner of that competition picking up the grand prize of a week's holiday in New York.

Sadly, Colin never got to enjoy his free week back at Pine Cliffs and the opportunity to challenge for the Big Apple break.

"I didn't know then that I was in the early stages of Parkinson's disease, although looking back I realise I was beginning to suffer with it. At the same time, Norma wasn't very well either, so in the end we didn't get to go back and I never got to play in the Weekly Winners' tournament."

But if Colin didn't get to return to Pine Cliffs, part of Pine Cliffs did come to him, in the form of a man called Jorge, who had been the shop manager there at the time of the Reads' resort stays. Years later, Jorge suddenly turned up in England. He'd lost his job at the resort golf course and, to use a golfing term, had then pitched up just a few miles from Colin's home village Podington, in nearby Harrold. Years earlier the two men had struck up regular conversations before and after Colin played his rounds of golf. Many of these chats had centred on the meaning of very English phrases. Surprisingly, though, it had been the Portuguese man who'd explained to the Englishman the origin of terms such as 'raining cats and dogs'. This shared interest in language also provides the background to a story Colin likes to tell:

"One morning I'd gone out for a round and had only played four or five holes when the wind got up and the rain, too. Normally I'd have played on, but the wind was really strong and the rain was lashing down, almost horizontal it was. So I gave up and walked back to the clubhouse. When I got there, I happened to meet Jorge and I told him that I'd packed up playing that day as it was sheeting down with rain. He then told me the Portuguese for 'sheeting down with rain'. I spoke pigeon Portuguese when I was at Pine Cliffs and now I'd learned another few words."

The following day Colin was back out on the nine-hole course. Again it was raining, if not quite hard enough this time to stop play. Continuing with his round, on the way he came across a couple of green keepers, and as he came up to them he decided to use the Portuguese term for 'sheeting down with rain' that Jorge had introduced him to the previous day, gesturing upwards to the rain as he did so.

The men's response was unexpected. They just looked at each other and laughed. Back at the clubhouse Colin again came across Jorge, who had a ready explanation for just why Colin's innocent-seeming remark in Portuguese had so amused the green keepers,

"Ah, that's my mistake," Jorge explained. "The phrase I gave you is what my wife, who speaks Brazilian Portuguese, uses. And its literal translation is 'putting the sheets on a bed'." No wonder it proved amusing to the green keepers.

A Developing Interest in Diamonds...

Another sporting interest in the early semi-retirement years was following the rise and rise of Rushden & Diamonds FC. Unlike his footballing father, Colin hadn't played the game, but having watched one Diamonds home match he was hooked. But just how, in the first place, did he come to find himself in the local team's stands, watching the local non-leaguers?

"I was driving down the A6 one day, from Kettering or somewhere, and I passed the club's stadium in Irthlingborough and saw these large posters stuck up on the side of one of the stands."

These posters were advertising forthcoming fixtures, and, before he knew it, Colin was a spectator as the newly formed club, heavily backed by its wealthy chairman Max Griggs, embarked on a decade of success that began with promotion from the Southern League Midland Division and culminated, at the end of the 2002–03 season, with yet another promotion, this time as champions of Football League Division Three.

"I used to go with one of my friends, Robert Langley, and other people, and I enjoyed the football. Every season was better than the one before, and in the end I even got a box at the Nene Park stadium. We'd also go to away games at big clubs like West Ham, Leeds and Coventry. And in 2002 we went to the Millennium Stadium, Cardiff, when the team lost there to Cheltenham Town in a play-off final."

Even when the bubble burst, and Rushden & Diamonds fell into oblivion even more quickly than it had risen up through the leagues, Colin continued to follow the team. Sad at the way the club declined and then folded, he's happy to have been part of the club's meteoric rise because as he says, "We had some good times."

President Read Goes to Whittlesey

In 1996, just as Rushden & Diamonds FC were finding their feet, Colin was making his own mark at Rushden 1935, the town's Round Table club, so called because it was formed in 1935 (coincidentally the year Colin was born).

"My Round Table life was busy. Every year I did all sorts of things. I was about 44, I suppose, when I joined. I found it difficult to do much because I was running the garden centre, but I kept on going with it and ended up being president, area chairman, on the district membership committee and at one stage setting up a new club at Sandy.

"When you're in a Round Table club, you all try to do everything that you can. It's not the case that the best man gets the job because everyone does their bit and gets involved. But I was renowned for my public speaking, and so I was out and about a lot, talking to various groups in the area."

One speaking 'gig' took place at the Round Table club in the small Fenland market town of Whittlesey near Peterborough. Beginning his speech there, Colin had got no further than thanking everyone for their sterling efforts in raising funds when he was suddenly cut off in mid-sentence.

"I'd just got going when the door behind me burst open and two men dressed in Home Guard uniforms rushed in with a blanket, which they threw over my head before bundling me outside. Meanwhile, everyone in the audience were killing themselves laughing!"

Soon 'released' by the pranksters, there was yet another surprise in store for the Rushden Round Tabler. Colin was presented with a gift in the form of a large cardboard box when he finished his speech. It was late at night by then, so the box was put unopened into the back of the car taking Colin back to Podington. Once home, he put his gift, still unopened, on top of the washing machine and went to bed. The next morning Norma was in the laundry room when she called out to Colin to ask him what was in the box she'd found there—a box from which odd sounds were emanating.

Curious now, husband and wife opened the box only to find that it contained a live cockerel! This practical joke cracked by the Whittlesey Rotary Club members, Colin took as a sign of the affection they had for him—"a bit of a laugh, really"—a warmth that later saw him receive a cherished award from that club.

"I was actually made an honorary member by them, as well as three other Round Table clubs, so that club and the others must have enjoyed my company as much as I enjoyed theirs."

At the age of 47, in 1982, Colin graduated from the Round Table to the Rotary Club of Rushden, the parent club of which was the larger Kettering group. Colin refers with pride to the large amount of money Rushden Rotary Club raised for charity and to the huge global impact made then and now by the wider movement's Rotary Foundation Charity, which includes a collaborative partnership with the Bill & Melinda Gates Foundation. This sees the organisation, set up by the Microsoft founder and his wife, donate $2 for every $1 contributed by the foundation towards the eradication of polio. Colin was the club's president from 1996 to 1997.

More Foreign Travels

In the late 1990s and on into the early years of the twenty-first century, a regular feature of Colin and Norma's life together was the foreign travel that resulted from belonging to the International Garden Centre Association.

"We were already a paid-up member of the Garden Centre Association, and over the years we won all its awards, including Garden Centre of the Year on three occasions, which was a real honour. Anyway, eventually we were invited to join the IGCA."

In 1996 the couple's South African adventure—baboons and all—had been their first trip abroad to take in an International Garden Centre Association congress, a week-long affair in late summer/early autumn that, still today, combines formalities (delegates electing officials and discussing matters arising), with fact finding (taking in visits to local garden centres) and visits to local places of interest.

After their trip to the southern tip of the African continent, the next foreign IGCA congress that Colin and Norma attended was in Ireland. Colin has few recollections of this stay spanning Dublin and Limerick, but those he does have are both unusual and amusing:

"I remember it was dark, dark when we arrived and as we, the British contingent, were driven in our coach to a special event that was being put on. No idea where it was, that event, but I do know the driveway was lit up by floodlights and the place itself was a lovely big country house. It was a tremendous affair with all these models walking around the place on stilts!"

Along with his 'Good enough isn't' catchphrase, as mentioned another recurring mantra for Colin centred on picking up one beneficial idea from each foreign trip he went on.

This had originally come out of a conversation with his old friend, Peter Neville, who, when the topic of travelling abroad came up, had said to Colin, "Come back with one good idea—and make it happen!" And so, while the visit to Ireland has few memories, there was the insight he gained into the "different styles of promotion" Irish garden centres used to market themselves and their wares.

The following year (2000), Munich was the host city for the IGCA congress. If Ireland was "dark", Germany was "very big". Big garden centres, at least, which for all their size didn't, in Colin's opinion, "achieve the class our centres seem to achieve". Smaller, but no more impressive, were the Christmas displays he saw in German garden centres.

"Ours were about 20 times bigger than the ones we saw there—and much better, too. I think, generally, we showed other people the way," he says.

But if German garden centres came up short in Colin's eyes, there was one attraction that did hit the mark for both Mr and Mrs Read. This they came across in Heidelberg, a town in one of the warmest parts of Germany that is renowned among horticulturalists for the unusual plants grown there. However, what caught their attention was not the town's flora but the superb Christmas market they visited.

International Incident in the White House

The following year's congress was held in the USA with three cities on the 2001 itinerary: New York, Baltimore and Washington DC. The trip was full of highlights for Colin and Norma, but most memorable for Colin was an episode that occurred in the American capital. The day of the episode started out straightforwardly enough with a coach load of IGCA delegates setting off for a nursery on the outskirts of Washington. Then, as Colin explains, the destination was changed. "We were travelling along a highway when one of the trip organisers made an announcement: 'Ladies and gentlemen, I know you thought you were going to a nursery today but we're actually going to The White House.' As it happened, we were already very close by and so, a few minutes later, the coach arrived at The White House gates and we were waved in."

Once inside, the group was taken on a tour of the building, seeing ordinary and extraordinary sights, the latter including a room full of saddles. Obviously security was tight.

"We were kept huddled together like a group of schoolchildren. No wandering, no stepping off the main route, no nothing. Not that anyone would've thought to do anything as the security guards were all at least six foot six and wearing holsters with guns in them."

The high security presence did not detract too much from the party's enjoyment of the tour, though, which took in features like the presidential running track and walks along corridors and past rooms lined with an impressive collection of statues, certificates, photographs and other artefacts. It was while the group was looking intently at some of these objects that one of the party sidled up to the tour organiser with a question he needed an urgent answer to. That person was Colin, and the question he posed was, "Can you ask one of the security men where I can go to the loo?"

Dave, the tour leader, put the question to the nearest security official, whose response was a loud and emphatic refusal. Seeing this, Colin stressed that he couldn't hold out much longer. On hearing this the security officer reluctantly relented, ordering a junior officer to 'Take this guy to the john!'. Colin was then marched off through a room where he heard office staff talking to themselves and asking 'Who's that guy?'. Then, when the toilet was finally reached, he was told by his escort to go into a cubicle. Once he was inside, the security man wedged his foot between the door and the frame so that the door couldn't be shut and locked. Even then there was no let-up:

Security officer (impatiently): Are you finished in there?
Colin (flustered): No, no.
Security officer (insistently): Come on, man. Hurry up!

Relieving himself just as fast as he could, the unwelcome toilet visitor was then swiftly marched back to join Norma and the rest of the party as they finished their White House tour.

Not all the memories of this American trip in September 2001 were so unexpected or so light-hearted, however. Visiting New York, one recollection from that part of the tour is poignant and sobering.

"We enjoyed a trip seeing the sights of the city which took in the Twin Towers. And, of course, we were there just a few days before those planes crashed into them on 9/11."

Outside The White House, Washington

The Last Congress

Colin and Norma's final foreign jaunt on IGCA business took place in 2003, the couple landing in Switzerland on 25 August. The main congress meetings that year were held in Bern, but what Colin remembers most vividly about the six-day stay was the time spent high up in the Swiss Alps, 2,570 metres above sea level at a remote location known, in English, as the Cadlimo Huts. This venue, lyrically described as the Gate to the South, provoked a mixed response, however.

"I seem to remember there were around 150 to 200 huts across the Alps for people to rest up in, in the event of an accident or bad weather. Anyway, it was decided that the committee of a dozen or so delegates, plus some of their partners, would hold a meeting at the Cadlimo Huts, which were self-sufficient in every respect for about a month."

Colin found the ascent to the huts relatively easy and enjoyed the spectacular view as the group climbed higher and higher. What he found at the end of the walk was less appealing, even if the view of long-horned goats and distant mountain peaks were exceptional. There, on a rocky outcrop, were a couple of buildings set side by side, each as basic as the other. No running hot water, of course, while even the cold water had to be collected from a nearby spring which flowed down the mountainside. And Colin's thoughts on sleeping two nights in his Alpine cabin?

"Awful! Couldn't wait to get back to the hotel," he says, adding, "We were only there two nights, but it felt like two weeks!"

Britain in Bloom

Colin's involvements with the IGCA, which took him, at different times, to events and meetings across four continents, also culminated in the association conferring one final honour on him.

Except that it wasn't actually conferred, as Colin explains: "In 2004, I was the president elect and was due to be formally sworn in at the international congress that was taking place in Auckland. I'd got the ticket to New Zealand, I'd got the cap and everything, but unfortunately when we were due to fly out Norma wasn't too well. I felt well enough in myself to have gone on my own, but I wouldn't have been happy with that and so I didn't go. And because of that I never did get to be the IGCA president."

Back home in the UK, Colin also filled a long-standing role as a member of the GCA. He was elected to the board, attending formal meetings at various grand buildings in London such as the Institution of Civil Engineers in London. These focused on burning industry issues, such as the unbalancing effect of a series of amalgamations of garden centres affiliated to the GCA, in addition to organising the association's annual conferences.

Eventually, Colin's high standing in horticultural circles saw him further recognised when he was contacted by the Britain in Bloom organisers. Asked to be a regional judge, he was only too pleased to accept.

"Obviously somebody had recommended me and I got this letter come through from Britain in Bloom. I really cherish something like that," he says.

Assigned judging duties in nearby counties, including towns in Leicestershire and Nottinghamshire, Colin fulfilled this honorary role for five years, along the way assessing everything from allotments to council flower beds, from individual gardens to municipal parks. He also encountered plenty of unexpected displays and situations. For instance, on one occasion Colin was told that a visit to Nottingham to assess city displays had been turned into a group outing for an army of councillors. Forewarned, he decided to take son Philip along for company and moral support.

"A number of councils had a habit of lining up councillors to join the Britain in Bloom judge, but in Nottingham they even laid on a double-decker bus. So there we were being driven through the local streets and they're all going 'What's he saying? What's he saying?'.

"Then, at one point, we went down this dual carriageway, and on the central reservation there's roses growing. Beautiful roses, really lovely display. So when I saw this display I said to the councillor next to me, in the loudest, most authoritative voice I could, 'What an effort you've put in to do that. It's wonderful!' Then I asked him how the outward-facing branches of the rose bushes were pruned, adding, 'You must have an army to do all that pruning.'

"He laughed, and all the other councillors on the coach laughed and then said, 'We use flower mowers.'

"I just stared at him and told him, 'You don't do that to roses!'

"And his reply was, 'Well, *we* do.' I'd never ever heard of people cutting plants that way, using the same awful tools that are used to cut hedgerows."

Some allotments in the city also provoked mixed feelings: they were well maintained, but were surrounded by high, unattractive and stark barbed-wire fencing. Despite these curiosities, Colin enjoyed his time as a Britain in Bloom judge, with his last mission taking him to the Nottinghamshire town of Newark-on-Trent, where he was joined not by councillors but by local press photographers. Their presence was just as unwanted, however.

"I was with the Britain in Bloom girl at about 10.30 on the day I was due to do my judging when she suddenly said, 'I hope you don't mind, Mr Read, but we've invited the press to join us.' The girl then took me round on foot to see the spots in Newark to be judged. So there we were, about an hour-and-a-half in, when this photographer turned up, and he didn't want to take pictures of the plants; he just wanted to take a picture of the judge doing his job.

"That made me quite annoyed, so I turned to the girl who was my escort and said, 'I've come here to judge, so I just want to be allowed to do that. This isn't about the press, it's for me to see the exhibits and assess them.' After that I finished judging what I had to judge just as quickly as I could.

"And do you know something? I was never invited to be a Britain in Bloom judge again!"

Health Concerns

One day in 2001 Colin was in a Bristol hotel room with wife Norma, looking forward to a GCA conference which was being held in the hotel. Beginning to get himself ready for the occasion, he went to have a shower. This everyday action on this day proved to be anything but routine.

"I stood in the shower cubicle and then, when I looked up at the ceiling, I couldn't see it properly; it kept disappearing. So I leant against the side of the cubicle and thought maybe I'd had too much to drink that day. Then I went back to the bedroom and told Norma what had happened. She thought I should stay in our room and go to bed, but I said, 'No, I'm all right,' and got ready to join the fun downstairs."

Still feeling a "bit giddy", Colin had not long met up with his fellow GCA members and their partners when he was offered a drink by a waiter. Taking a glass of wine, Colin promptly spilt it before falling in a heap on the floor.

An ambulance was called and he was rushed off to the Bristol Royal Infirmary. There he spent the night before being driven back to Podington the following morning. Once there he was booked in for a scan.

"The scan showed that I'd had a mini stroke and that there was a slight scarring on the brain. My brain cleverly managed to take over the scarred area's responsibilities, as it were, and after about six weeks I was back to normal, although I did have to take a statin, a cholesterol-lowering drug, and I still take it now".

Thankfully, there were no further stroke episodes, but another health issue was lying in wait just over the horizon. This issue was Parkinson's disease, a condition that, unlike the earlier mini stroke, was not promptly diagnosed. With what Colin now knows, this, he believes, is not unusual.

"Most people who get Parkinson's don't know they've got it, and not even the people who run Parkinson's support organisations can always tell you that you have it. I think there are roughly 159,000 people in the UK that have the disease, and the fact is there are so many possible symptoms."

In his own case, the first sign that something was wrong was a slight shaking in the arms and hands, a mannerism that the family quickly picked up on. This shaking behaviour, though, was not what led Colin to be sitting one day before Dr Petredes at the Blackberry Clinic in Milton Keynes. He'd been suffering with pains in his neck and shoulders, but when the doctor looked at the results of a scan he'd ordered, he saw something that led him to contact his patient's GP. The GP then referred Colin to a consultant specialising in Parkinson's disease.

"She was a lady called Dr Hubbard and she started doing tests on me. These went on for quite some time until, at one of my appointments with her, I heard her say to one of her assistants, 'I think Mr Read has Parkinson's.' That was maybe two-and-a-half years after the scan I'd had at the Blackberry Clinic."

At that stage, Colin had begun to notice changes in what he could do and how he felt. Before his condition had been confirmed, and drugs had been prescribed, he found he could still walk quite quickly and in a straight line. But, by the time in 2013 that Dr Hubbard had diagnosed Parkinson's disease, he could walk okay but had real difficulty changing direction. Medication has helped combat this and addressed Colin's shaking spasms. It's also assisted where balance is concerned, while exercises, both physical and mental, have also formed part of the treatment regime, with the result, for example, that he's able to partially control the shaking in his arms and legs.

"I can persuade myself to relax when I'm sitting talking with someone. I also find that if I sit up and look at the person I'm talking with I can actually speak better as well. So I can speak better and I don't shake."

Of course, there was never any likelihood of Colin taking the diagnosis of Parkinson's lying down. Instead, he's raised thousands of pounds for Parkinson's UK, calling on his established Rotary Club and business contacts (and others besides) to raise money for the cause. It was as a result of these fund-raising efforts that, in March 2015, Colin was able to present a cheque for £1,500 to the charity, explaining as he did so that "raising funds is my way to help contribute and make a difference".

Another Honour Comes Colin's Way

In his mid-seventies, at a time when many are happy to rest on their laurels, Colin joined an elite and august organisation, a membership that opened doors on some interesting experiences, some grand, some not. The organisation was the Worshipful Company of Gardeners, a London guild with origins dating back to the fourteenth century. Today, it is one of 66 such guilds, which include those with medieval roots (merchant tailors, needle makers, wheelwrights), unusual guilds (makers of playing cards, water conservators) and thoroughly modern ones (including air pilots and information technologists). For Colin, his connection with the gardeners' guild began with a visit to the Houses of Parliament.

"I'd gone there on a Garden Centre Association tour, and while I was on the trip I found out that a number of the other committee members that I was with that day were also members of the gardeners' livery organisation. I got talking to them about the guild, and they ended up proposing me as a member. A short time later I was interviewed and accepted as a member."

Colin took an immediate shine to the Worshipful Company of Gardeners, but while he has played his part in formal guild affairs, it's been the social, informal events—such as a visit to the National Memorial Arboretum at Alrewas, near Lichfield—that he's enjoyed most.

"It was an honour to be invited to join the company, and then, when I got involved, I just wished I'd become a member earlier because there are some lovely things you get to see and do thanks to the company—the Lord Mayor's Show, trips to the arboretum and other interesting places."

It was through the Worshipful Company of Gardeners of London that, in 2010, Colin was awarded the prestigious Freedom of the City of London. Although this came about

At the Worshipful Company of Gardeners, Colin having
received his membership certificate and robe

Colin & Norma at Mansion House, London, representing
the Worshipful Company of Gardeners

through Colin's association with the livery company, it is not an honour that every liveryman is granted.

Family Delights

In his eighties now, Colin and devoted wife Norma spend much of their time enjoying their retirement in the Podington house they've called home for more than four decades. Their garden, with its greenhouses, shrubs and flowers, and mix of design features and ornaments, is both immaculate and varied and a source of continuing pleasure. And then there's the love, support and delights provided by their large and still local family.

Coincidentally, sons Philip and Jonathan married two sisters they met through their Young Farmers' involvement. Philip married the younger sister, Helen Dunmore, while Jonathan married her older sister, Ruth. There's another coincidence, too, which is that both couples have three children. Surprisingly, perhaps, not one of Colin and Norma's grandchildren has yet developed a passion for plants. That noted, their grandfather talks proudly about how each, in his or her own distinctive way, is excelling.

"Philip and Helen's oldest child is Hannah, who's in her twenties. She is clever and very structured and is about to start a masters degree. Their middle child, Harry, loves his acting and is interested in film production. And then there's young Molly, who's still at school working towards her GCSEs and is a good gymnast.

"Jonathan and Ruth, on the other hand, have three boys: William's a computer boffin like his father and is at university. He's even written software programs for the university to use. The middle son, Arthur, wants to be a veterinary nurse and is studying at Moulton College. And then there's Harvey, who's really good at English."

The Reluctant Sale of the Garden Centre

By mid-2014, Colin, who was by then showing more signs of Parkinson's, had transferred the administration of the business and the overall operation of the garden centre to his sons, Philip and Jonathan.

Not long afterwards, the family were persuaded to attend the Garden Centre Association annual awards and were thrilled to receive the 'Garden Centre of the Year' award, which put the icing on the cake for the thriving business. This award was obviously the jam that attracted the fly as the family received a good offer for the business which was accepted, and the garden centre was sold.

However, the decision to sell the family business, which had been built up and run successfully as a garden-centre enterprise for 33 long years, Colin admits, was the most difficult decision the family has ever taken.

But when an agreement was reached to sell, and the terms of the sale had been negotiated, all that was left to do was to exchange contracts.

Then, finally, with a heavy heart, the Reads handed over the keys to their 6,000-square-metre site with its 2,500-square-metre shop and plant area containing more than 9,000 varieties.

That same day, the Reads issued a press release that had, at its heart, the following statement:

We are proud of what we built at Podington and proud that we have always ensured any developments had our customers in mind. We would like to thank our wonderful team for all they have done for us.

Married for 60 Years… & Counting!

In November 2015, less than a year after the sale of Podington Garden Centre, Colin turned 80. The occasion was marked by a family get-together, complete with children and grandchildren, at his High Street home. Then, in February 2017, Colin and Norma celebrated their 60th wedding anniversary. To celebrate this latest marital milestone, the couple enjoyed another family party in Podington. A short time later, the occasion was marked by the receipt of a special card.

It is a treasured note from the Queen, that same royal lady, of course, who one sunny morning, many years ago, stopped to accept a bouquet of flowers at the entrance to Podington Garden Centre.

This is the place that is now an imposing reminder of how Colin Read, and his close knit family, so successfully built, established and developed their long-running, award-winning business, and in so doing proved, over and over, that, for Colin and the Read family, 'Good enough isn't' but being the best at what you do certainly is.

I am so pleased to know that you celebrated your Diamond Wedding anniversary on 16th February, 2017. I send my congratulations and best wishes to you for such a special occasion.

Elizabeth R

Mr. and Mrs. Colin Read